SCENARIO BOOK

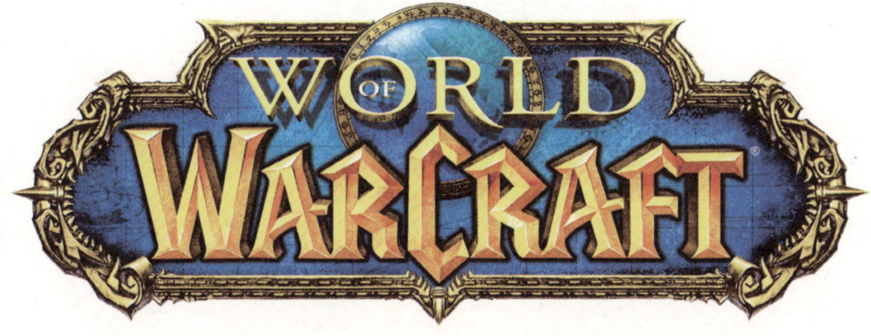

UNSHACKLED

AN ESCAPE ROOM BOX

Additional Puzzles by: Helen Cheng
Edited by: Allison Avalon Irons, Chloe Fraboni
Designed by: Betsy Peterschmidt
Produced by: Derek Rosenberg
Lore Consultation by: Sean Copeland

BLIZZARD ENTERTAINMENT
Vice President, Consumer Products: Matthew Beecher
Director, Consumer Products, Publishing: Byron Parnell
Associate Publishing Manager: Derek Rosenberg
Director, Manufacturing: Anna Wan
Senior Director, Story and Franchise Development: David Seeholzer
Senior Producer: Brianne Messina
Lead Editor: Chloe Fraboni
Editor: Allison Avalon Irons
Book Art & Design Manager: Betsy Peterschmidt
Historian Supervisor: Sean Copeland
Senior Historian: Justin Parker
Associate Historian: Madi Buckingham

TITAN BOOKS
A division of Titan Publishing Group Ltd
144 Southwark Street. London SE1 0UP
www.titanbooks.com
Find us on Facebook: www.facebook.com/titanbooks
Follow us on Twitter: @TitanBooks
A CIP catalogue record for this title is available
from the British Library.

ISBN barcode: 978-1-7890-9888-4
Manufactured in China

Print run 10 9 8 7 6 5 4 3 2 1

PERIL IN UN'GORO CRATER

DIFFICULTY

Adventurers from the Horde and Alliance determined to test their mettle set forth into Un'Goro Crater. When plans go awry and the group is beset by the terrifying devilsaur King Mosh, the lost heroes must follow encoded clues left by Brann Bronzebeard to escape the crater with their lives!

UNIQUE RULE: BLOODPETALS

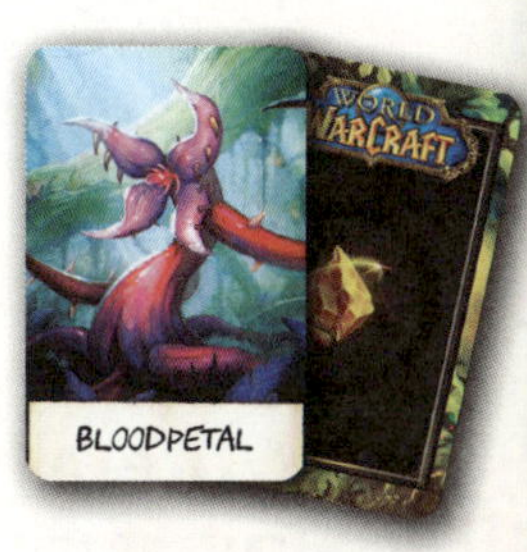

Un'Goro Crater is full of walking plants covered with thorns called **bloodpetals**. While lovely from a distance, these photosynthesizing menaces secrete a paralyzing toxin sure to stop any adventurer in their tracks. The Game Master must warn the players that the bloodpetals exist but may choose not to reveal the effects the cards might have until triggered.

When setting up, the GM hides the bloodpetal cards around the game space in addition to the puzzle cards. The bloodpetal cards have no specific markings on their backs. When a hero discovers a bloodpetal card, they must keep it with them. They cannot put the card back. No effect triggers, and the GM does not provide any information about the card. When the same hero has three bloodpetal cards, they are inflicted with a **bloodpetal toxin effect** chosen by the GM from the list on page 5.

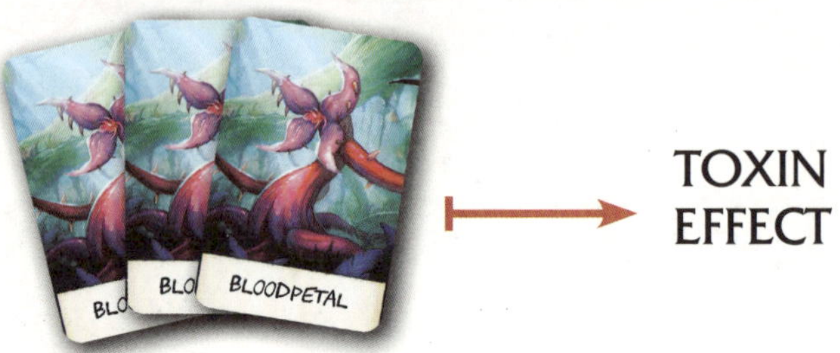

The heroes must be very careful while searching the room and communicate with each other so that a person who has already found a pair of bloodpetal cards does not find one too many!

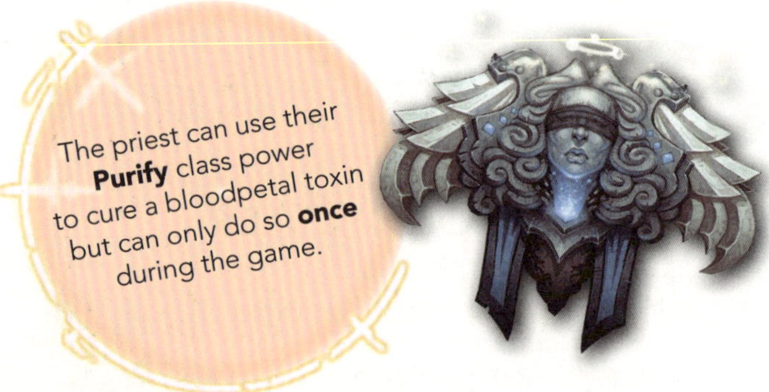

The priest can use their **Purify** class power to cure a bloodpetal toxin but can only do so **once** during the game.

WHAT HAPPENS AFTER A PLAYER FINDS THREE BLOODPETAL CARDS?

The player gives the GM the three bloodpetal cards. The GM then chooses a toxin effect for the player to be inflicted with. If the same player finds another three bloodpetal cards, they can get another toxin effect.

The GM may vary the number of bloodpetal cards used for this scenario according to the number of heroes.

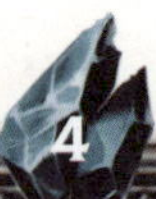

<table>
<tr><td align="center">2 HEROES</td><td align="center">3 – 5 HEROES</td></tr>
<tr><td align="center">Hide 9 bloodpetal cards</td><td align="center">Hide 15 bloodpetal cards</td></tr>
</table>

Bloodpetal Toxin Effects:

- The hero cannot talk for 5 minutes.

- The hero must keep one foot firmly on the ground and can only pivot around that position for 5 minutes.

- One minute is automatically removed from the game timer.

SCENARIO EVENTS

The events below allow the Game Master to increase the difficulty of the game and add their own narrative flavor to the scenario's story. Events can be triggered whenever the GM desires.

Predator: A hungry devilsaur passes nearby! Sudden movements will make the creature aggressive. The players must freeze in place and not move for 30 seconds. If one of the players fails and moves, their arm is bitten by the devilsaur. The player suffers a penalty that prevents them from moving their dominant arm for 5 minutes.

Budding: The GM asks the players to close their eyes and quickly replaces some of the bloodpetal cards that were already found.

Pollination: A huge, brightly colored plant just exhaled a cloud of spores. The heroes must hold their breath for 30 seconds. The player(s) who fail to do so get a 5-minute penalty that plunges them into confusion and forces them to mix up words in their sentences.

SETTING UP THE SCENARIO

This scenario uses cards 1 to 53 and documents "Potion of Massive Nausea" and "About Dinosaurs."

LEAVE THESE CARDS VISIBLE	GM KEEPS THESE CARDS IN THEIR HANDS	HIDE THESE CARDS	HIDE THESE CARDS IN CHALLENGING PLACES
2, 6, 10, 12, 14, 32, 35, 42	1, 7, 13, 18, 19, 22, 26, 28, 29, 30, 31, 37, 38, 39, 40, 41, 45, 46, 48, 50, 51, 52, 53; "Potion of Massive Nausea" document, "About Dinosaurs" document	3, 4, 5, 8, 11, 17, 23, 24, 27, 33, 34, 43, 44	9, 15, 16, 20, 21, 25, 36, 47, 49

In total, there are 22 cards to hide (plus up to 15 bloodpetal cards), 8 to leave visible, and 23 for the GM to keep in hand.

Once the setup is complete, the Game Master may ask the players to enter the game space. Get creative and decorate your game space if you are feeling ambitious! Scan the included QR code to acquire the accompanying scenario soundtrack.

INTRODUCTION

GM: Read the following to the players before starting the game.

"A brightly colored parrot flies over the camp you just set up. It screeches. Some of you are startled. But there are scarier things in Un'Goro Crater, I can tell you.

"You are members of the Horde and the Alliance on a peaceful expedition to explore the wilderness of Un'Goro Crater. The journey so far has filled you with wonder. Thick vegetation and time-lost plants are teeming all around you. The jungle shudders with the sounds of hundreds of creatures big and small, docile and dangerous."

GM: Explain that the heroes should call out bloodpetal cards as they find them.

"You choose to stay close to your group, clinging tightly to your map. You're not afraid, just cautious, right? Grand explorers should never be afraid!

"The ground trembles beneath your feet. A massive devilsaur tears through the trees with a deafening roar. A huge mouth with rows of fangs longer than your arms gnashes at your group with a terrible crunch. Only one devilsaur was said to be this menacing, locally called King Mosh. You are all knocked off your feet and thrown head over heels. Your backpacks and provisions are useless to you now as Mosh ravages them.

"Dazed, you hide as best you can, leaving Mosh free to furiously trample your camp. Fortunately, he could not find your group among the dense leaves. Other animals are attracted to the remains of the camp: a beautiful parrot, an opportunistic raptor, likely more. After coming to your senses, you search what is left of the camp and find only a **piece of the map** that had guided you into the crater. How are you possibly going to get out now?"

GM: Give the heroes card 18 and read the following out loud.

"The rest of the map must be inside King Mosh or stolen by other creatures. There isn't much left of your bags or supplies. You'll have to search for something else to help you. As you stumble around the torn tent and splintered wood, you find a weathered bag nailed to a tree. Painted on the bag is the crest of the Explorers' League and the faded words 'In Case of Emergency.'"

GM: Give the heroes card 1 and read the following out loud.

"The noises around you suddenly get more threatening—and hungrier. You must find a way to leave the crater alive!"

GM: Start the timer and soundtrack for this scenario.

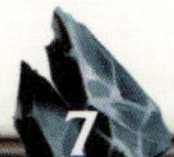

PUZZLE 1: THE EMERGENCY BAG

CARDS: 1, 2, 3, and 4

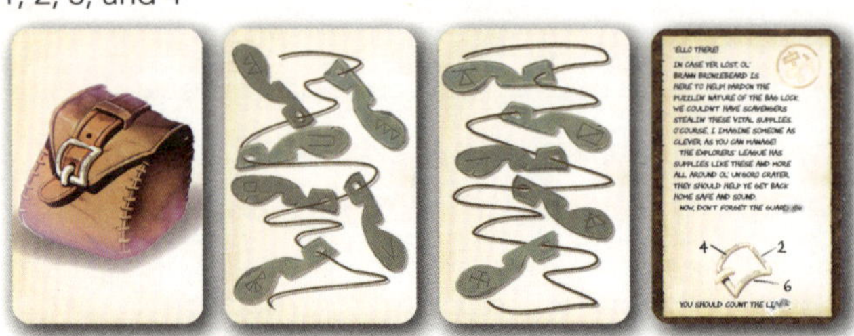

GM CLUES:

1. The shapes on the bag lock are very specific; is there something nearby that has similar shapes?

2. Somewhere, Brann must have written down how to open the emergency bag so he wouldn't forget.

3. It looks like something has been erased. Perhaps start there?

METHOD:

Once **both pieces of the necklace** with pendants are found, the heroes must realize which ones to use by using card 4, where they are advised to "**count**."

The heroes count the lines of each symbol and, still using card 4, correctly place the one that has two, then the one that has four, and another one that has six.

SOLUTION:

The heroes must tell the GM where each pendant goes in the lock. See illustration right.

When the players do so, the GM reads the following out loud.

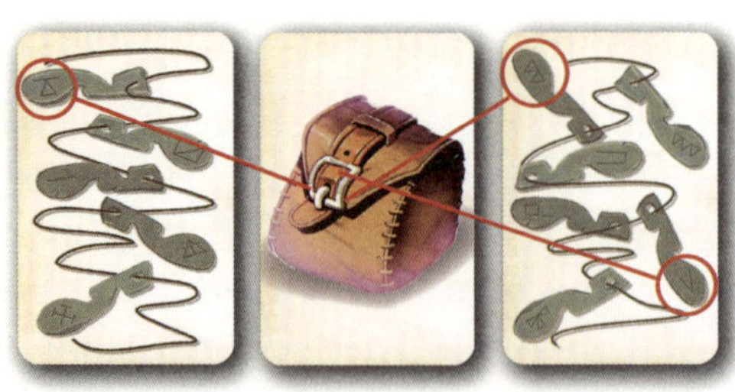

"You manage to open the emergency bag. As Brann feared, it seems that most of the supplies were taken. The only interesting thing left is a recipe for a potion to make a huge creature sick. You also find a tasty-looking worm."

GM: Give the heroes the "Potion of Massive Nausea" document and card 13, then read the following out loud.

"Perhaps you could use the concoction on King Mosh with the hope that he will spit out everything he swallowed, including the pieces of the crater map! But you will still need to find King Mosh and the ingredients needed for the recipe. While doing so, you might even find more supplies and guidance left by Brann and the Explorers' League. Currently you are standing at the edge of the camp. Your escape begins here."

GM: Give the heroes card 7.

PUZZLE 2: ON THE TRAIL OF KING MOSH

CARDS: 5, 6, 7, 8, 9, 10, 11, and 12

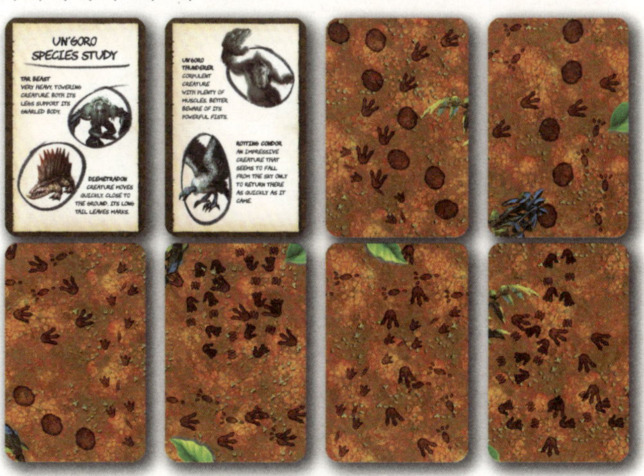

GM CLUES:

1 Try to focus on the common elements between the creatures and their environments.

2 There are several sets of tracks. What do Mosh's look like? Try eliminating the footsteps that can't be his.

METHOD:

By matching the natural elements, the heroes piece together part of the jungle with cards 7 through 12.

Cards 5 and 6 of the species study make it possible to deduce by elimination which footprints belong to Mosh.

SOLUTION:

The heroes retrace the path of Mosh.

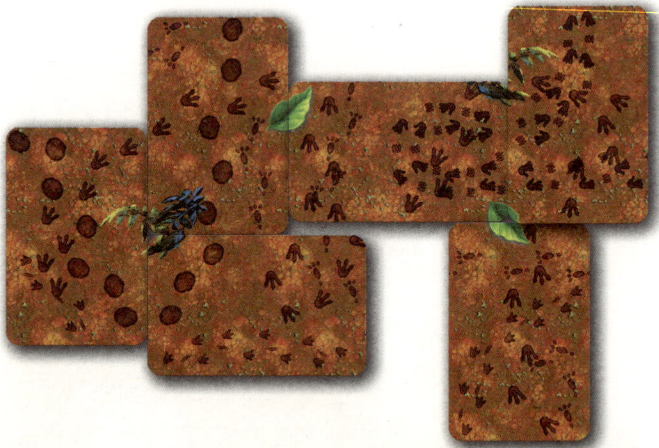

When they do so, the GM reads the following aloud.

> *"You discreetly follow Mosh's tracks and discover his nest. The devilsaur looks calm, so it's best not to disturb him before giving him the sickness potion."*

> GM: Give the heroes card 53.

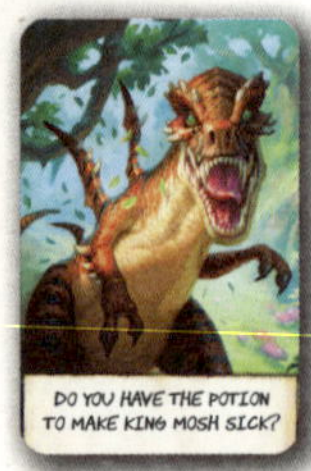

PUZZLE 3: KING MOSH'S MEAL

CARDS: 13, 14, 15, 16, 17, and the "Potion of Massive Nausea" document

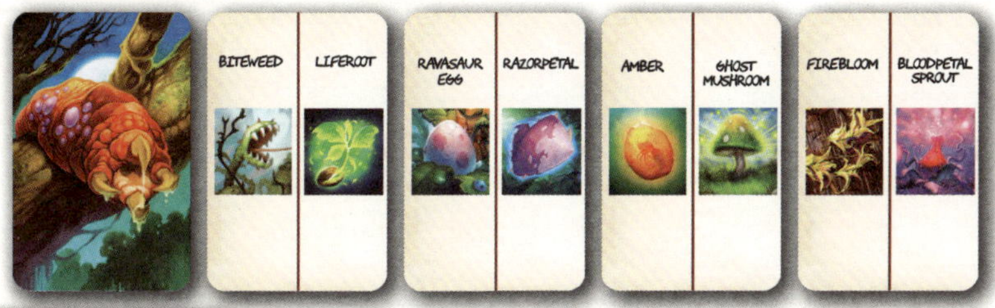

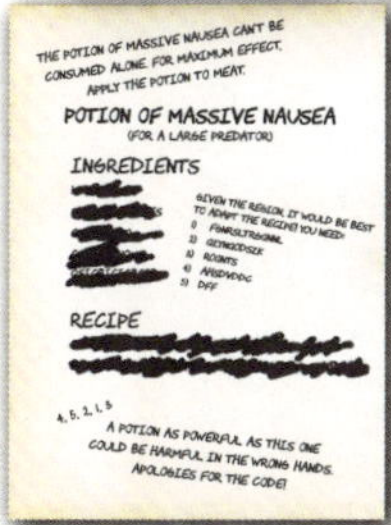

SIDE A

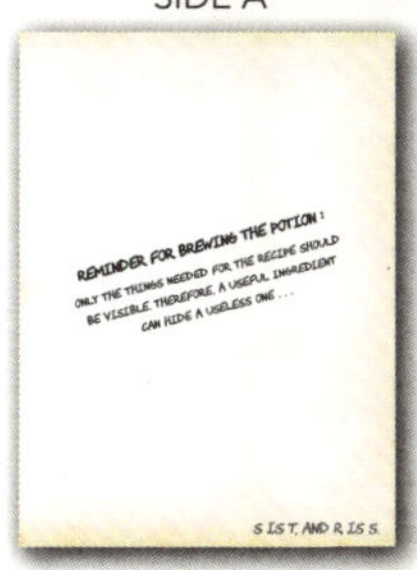

SIDE B

GM CLUES:

1. The coding used by the guide is a simple substitution code: one letter corresponds to another.

2. Overlay the ingredient cards to hide those that are not useful for the recipe.

METHOD:

The heroes translate the list of ingredients needed by substituting each encrypted letter for the letter following it in the alphabet: A becomes B, P becomes Q, etc. They get: ghost mushroom, razorpetal, sprout, biteweed, and egg—and realize this refers to the plants labeled on cards 14-17.

Cross referencing the number combination on the "Potion of Massive Nausea" document with the numbered list of ingredients, players must overlap cards 14-17 in the right order. The solution shows the correct ingredients in the correct order of the recipe: biteweed, ravasaur egg, razorpetal, ghost mushroom, and bloodpetal sprout.

SOLUTION:

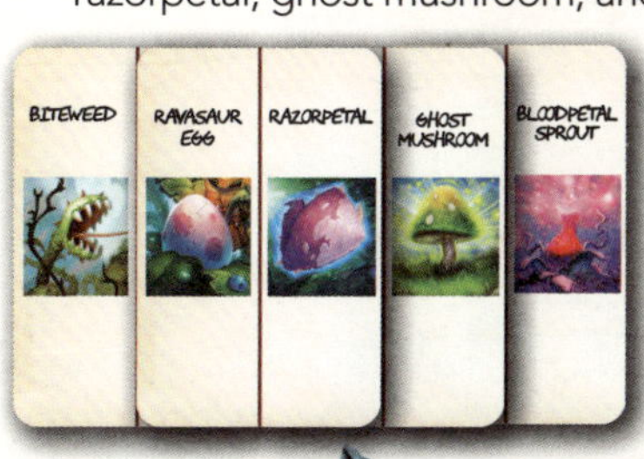

When heroes make the right recipe, the GM reads the following aloud.

"Once the potion is put on the meat, you leave it near Mosh's nest. The devilsaur does not take long to pounce on the piece of meat and devour it. Seconds later, he spits out shapeless clumps and flees, roaring as he goes. Among the unappetizing remains of Mosh's lunch, you find the map pouch with another piece of the map! You also find a piece of paper."

GM: Give the heroes card 19 and the "About Dinosaurs" document.

PUZZLE 4: THE MAP OF THE CRATER

CARDS: 18, 19, 20, and 21

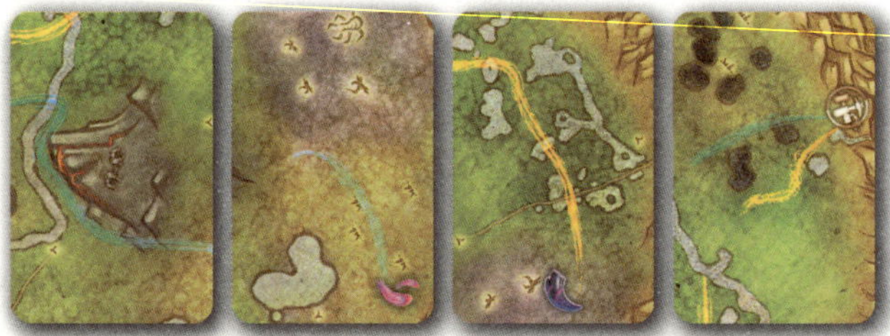

GM CLUE:

1 The cards may overlap each other.

METHOD:

The heroes simply piece together the map with the cards they have.

SOLUTION:

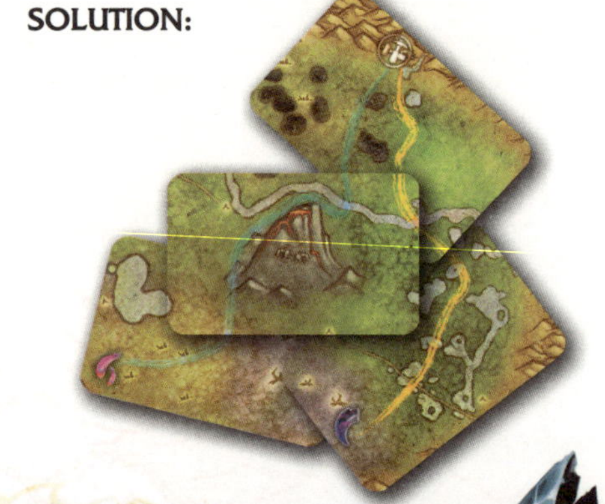

Once the heroes have pieced together the path, the GM reads the following aloud.

"With the parts of the map you have pieced together, you can see that the Explorers' League has surveyed two paths. With no other leads, you must explore the routes and try to find a way out of the crater. What direction will you choose?"

If the heroes decide to go to the location marked with a feather, read on to **puzzle 5**. For the location marked with a claw, read on to **puzzle 6**.

PUZZLE 5: BIRD BRAINS

GM: Read the following to the heroes.

"Instead of leaving the crater, you go deeper into the jungle and discover a dirty piece of paper."

GM: Give the heroes card 26.

"At the same time, a parrot with beautiful rainbow colors lands on a branch. You recognize it as the one who visited your camp after Mosh destroyed it. The parrot has something in its beak: a piece of the map! It gives you a haughty look, then flies away. You chase it but fail to keep up. Above your head, another smaller parrot lets out a cry. And another. And another."

GM: Give the heroes card 22.

CARDS: 22, 23, 24, 25, 26, and 27

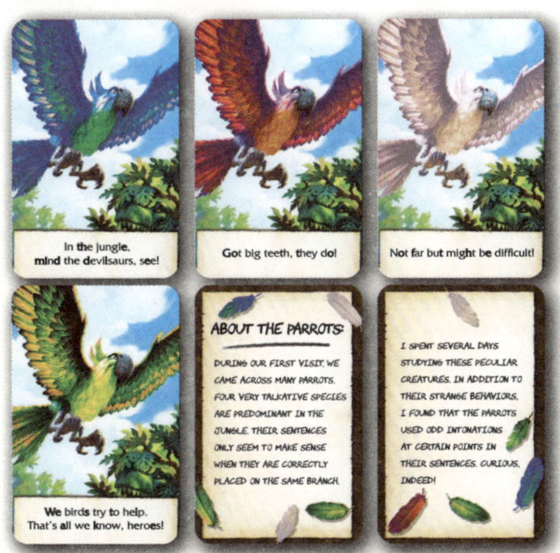

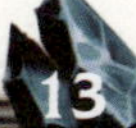

GM CLUES:

1 The number of feathers should help you correctly order the parrots.

2 Be attentive to what the parrots say. They seem to be hiding something in their sentences.

METHOD:

Based on the number of feathers on cards **26** and **27**, the heroes place the four parrots in the right order: red, blue, white, and green.

They then read each parrot's sentence and look for what might be hidden. For each one, some letters stand out, forming words:

Red parrot: **go to**

Blue parrot: **the middle**

White parrot: **of the**

Green parrot: **west lake**

SOLUTION:

Once the heroes have asnwered "Go to the middle of west lake," the GM reads the following aloud.

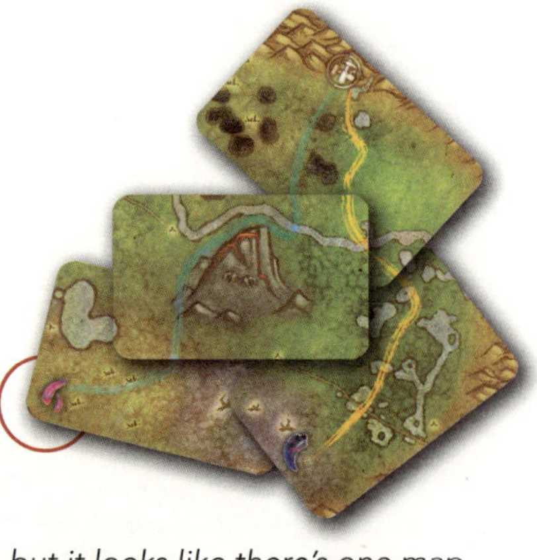

> "You reach the end of the blue path and discover the nest of the rainbow parrot. Among the multicolored feathers you find a curious crystal, along with another missing piece of the map. It seems to indicate the 'West Lake' the parrots referred to, but it looks like there's one map piece still missing."

> GM: Give the heroes card 38. If the heroes have not yet taken the path marked with a claw leading to Puzzle 6, read the following aloud.

> "You still do not know how to leave the crater. As you assess your situation, two raptors start chasing you, forcing you to run through the jungle. At the end of your mad dash, you find yourself in the middle of a wild area…"

Read on to **puzzle 6**.

If the players have explored both paths, they can now fully complete the Un'Goro map. Continue to page 17.

PUZZLE 6: SHARP TEMPERS

GM: Read the following aloud.

"The jungle is getting thicker and the sounds within more threatening. You feel like you're being watched—and you are. Several dinosaurs are moving through the foliage and steadily getting closer."

GM: Give the heroes cards 28, 29, 30, and 31.

"Your group seems to have trespassed on the dinosaurs' territory. You'll have to figure out how to soothe these terrifying creatures before you can pass safely through."

CARDS: 28, 29, 30, 31, 32, 33, 34, 36, and the "About Dinosaurs" document

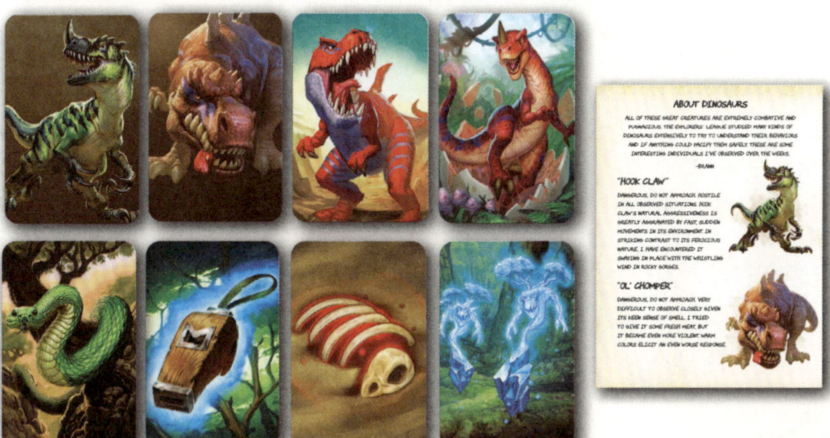

GM CLUES:

1. You must calm down each dinosaur with something specific.
2. Proceed by deduction and elimination; the study paper will help you.

3 You can use only one card per dinosaur, so pay attention to the arrangement.

4 Look at the cards you have not used yet; you may not need all the resources you have.

METHOD:

Once the four different dinosaurs have been found, the heroes seek out what can calm each of them down.

The study makes it possible to deduce:

"Hook Claw" is intrigued by whistling noises that remind it of the wind, so the whistle on card 33.

"Ol' Chomper" is calmed by cool colors, like the blue living mana on card 36.

"Gerald" is calmed down by bones, so card 34 would be correct.

"Clever Lad" gets along with other predators it can hunt with, like the snake on card 32.

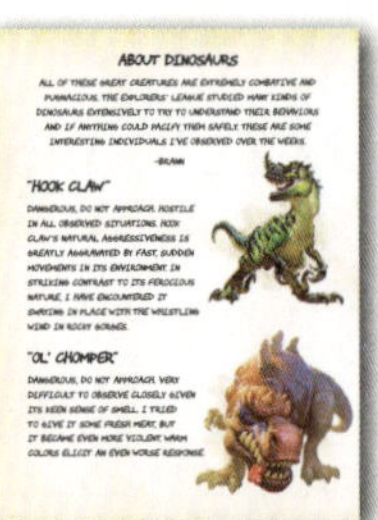

ABOUT DINOSAURS

ALL OF THESE GREAT CREATURES ARE EXTREMELY COMBATIVE AND PUGNACIOUS. THE EXPLORERS' LEAGUE STUDIED MANY KINDS OF DINOSAURS EXTENSIVELY TO TRY TO UNDERSTAND THEIR BEHAVIORS AND IF ANYTHING COULD PACIFY THEM SAFELY. THESE ARE SOME INTERESTING INDIVIDUALS I'VE OBSERVED OVER THE WEEKS.

-BRAM

"HOOK CLAW"

DANGEROUS, DO NOT APPROACH. HOSTILE IN ALL OBSERVED SITUATIONS. HOOK CLAW'S NATURAL AGGRESSIVENESS IS GREATLY AGGRAVATED BY FAST, SUDDEN MOVEMENTS IN ITS ENVIRONMENT. IN STRIKING CONTRAST TO ITS FEROCIOUS NATURE, I HAVE ENCOUNTERED IT SWAYING IN PLACE WITH THE WHISTLING WIND IN ROCKY GORGES.

"OL' CHOMPER"

DANGEROUS, DO NOT APPROACH. VERY DIFFICULT TO OBSERVE CLOSELY GIVEN ITS KEEN SENSE OF SMELL. I TRIED TO GIVE IT SOME FRESH MEAT, BUT IT BECAME EVEN MORE VIOLENT. WARM COLORS ELICIT AN EVEN WORSE RESPONSE.

SIDE A

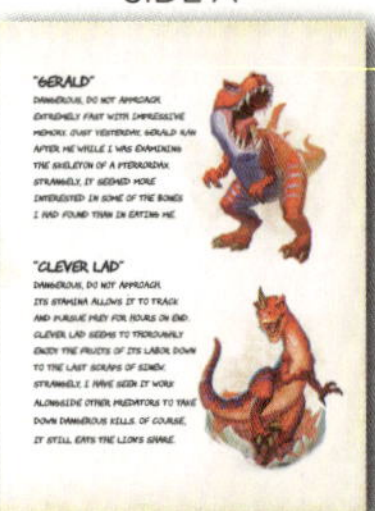

"GERALD"

DANGEROUS, DO NOT APPROACH. EXTREMELY FAST WITH IMPRESSIVE MEMORY. JUST YESTERDAY, GERALD RAN AFTER ME WHILE I WAS EXAMINING THE SKELETON OF A PTERRORIMAX. STRANGELY, IT SEEMED MORE INTERESTED IN SOME OF THE BONES I HAD FOUND THAN IN EATING ME.

"CLEVER LAD"

DANGEROUS, DO NOT APPROACH. ITS STAMINA ALLOWS IT TO TRACK AND PURSUE PREY FOR HOURS ON END. CLEVER LAD SEEMS TO THOROUGHLY ENJOY THE FRUITS OF ITS LABOR DOWN TO THE LAST SCRAPS OF SINEW. STRANGELY, I HAVE SEEN IT WORK ALONGSIDE OTHER PREDATORS TO TAKE DOWN DANGEROUS KILLS. OF COURSE, IT STILL EATS THE LION'S SHARE.

SIDE B

SOLUTION:

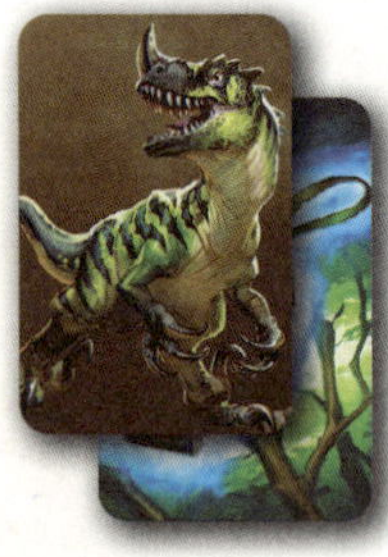 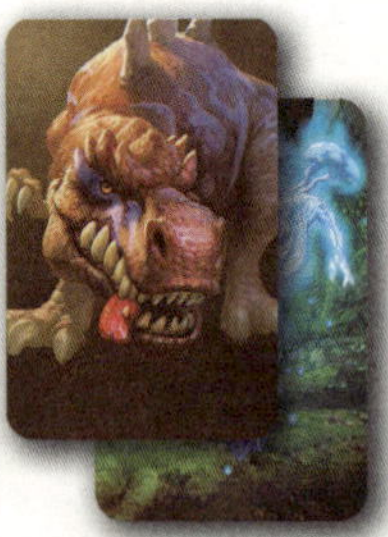 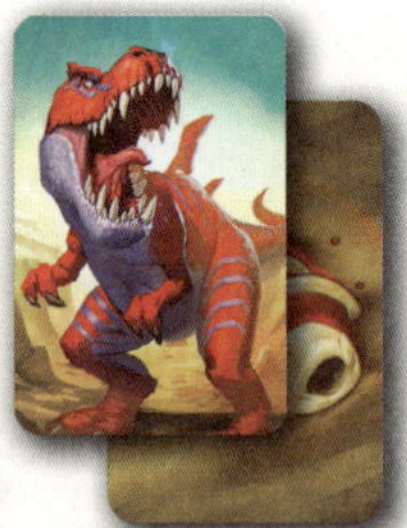 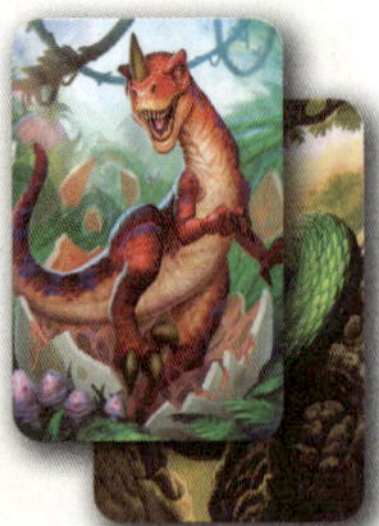

If the heroes make a mistake when they give their answer, the GM can apply the **Predator** event before reminding them to think carefully.

Once they have found the solution, the GM reads the following aloud.

"With the dinosaurs calmed down, you manage to make your way through their territory safely. As the trees clear, you find an old Explorers' League bag with a curious crystal inside. You also find a piece of your map pierced by a broken-off dinosaur claw."

GM: Give the heroes cards 37 and 46.

If the heroes have not yet taken the path marked with a feather leading to puzzle 6, the GM reads the following aloud.

"You still do not know how to leave the crater. As you assess your situation, a parrot flies over you, shrieking. Perhaps it is headed toward something interesting?"

Read on to **puzzle 5**.

If they have explored both paths, the heroes realize that they can complete the whole map of Un'Goro.

The heroes complete the map and discover another place that may help them escape Un'Goro Crater:

"With the map restored, you can now navigate your way to the west lake and, hopefully, to freedom. Unfortunately, as you make your way between vines and gigantic tree trunks, you are beset and taken prisoner by a group of pounders—gorillas. You are astonished at their advanced intelligence. You find yourself locked in a cage, kept shut by a curious lock."

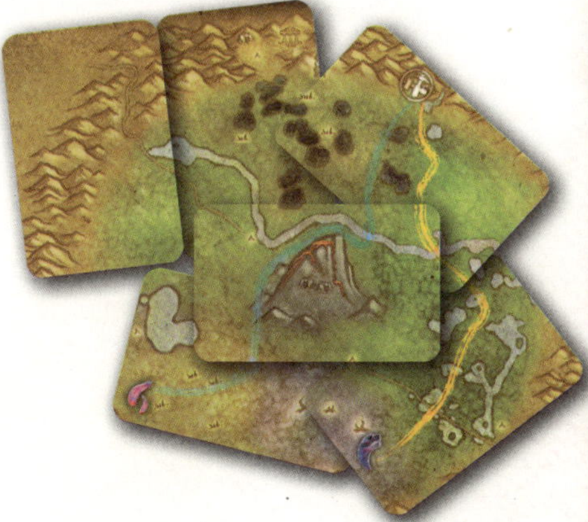

GM: Give the heroes card 40.

"Your jailer is a very young gorilla. He looks less ferocious than the others and has the remains of an Explorers' League bandana around his neck. After you get his attention, he draws something in the dirt. What could he want?"

GM: Give the heroes card 39.

PUZZLE 7: BEWARE THE GORILLAS!

CARDS: 35 and 39

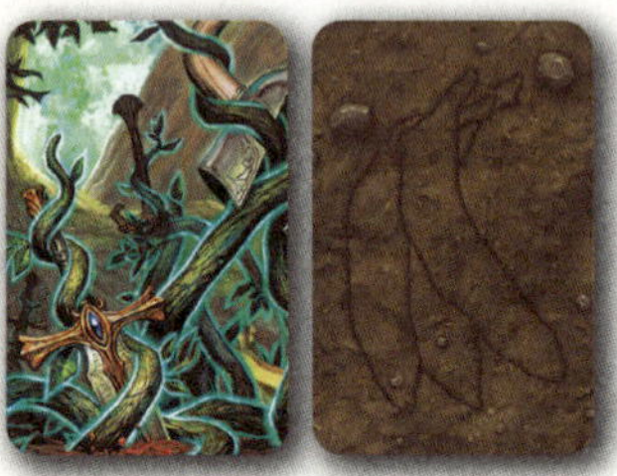

GM CLUE:

① Look at the young gorilla's drawing closely. Does it remind you of something you already came across?

METHOD:

The heroes must locate the banana hidden among the cards that were left visible to them.

SOLUTION:

They tell the GM that they want to use **card 35**—on which the fruit appears—with the young gorilla.

Once the heroes have found the solution, the GM reads the following aloud.

> *"The young gorilla grabs the fruit you give him and goes away to eat it on his own. He leaves behind a curious object that you pick up."*

> *GM: Give the heroes card 41.*

PUZZLE 8: OUT OF THE CAGE

CARDS: 40, 41, 42, 43, and 44

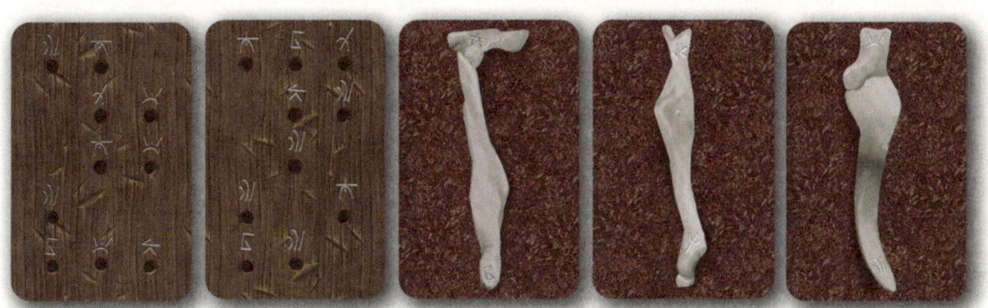

GM CLUES:

1. Can you see marks on the different bones?
2. Don't these look like keys?
3. Both ends of the key are essential.

METHOD:

Once they have cards 40 through 44, the heroes make the connection between the symbols on the bones and the strange lock.

When they realize they are keys, the heroes must figure out how they should be inserted into the lock.

They match the symbol on one end and rotate the card to find the symbol that matches the opposite end.

SOLUTION:

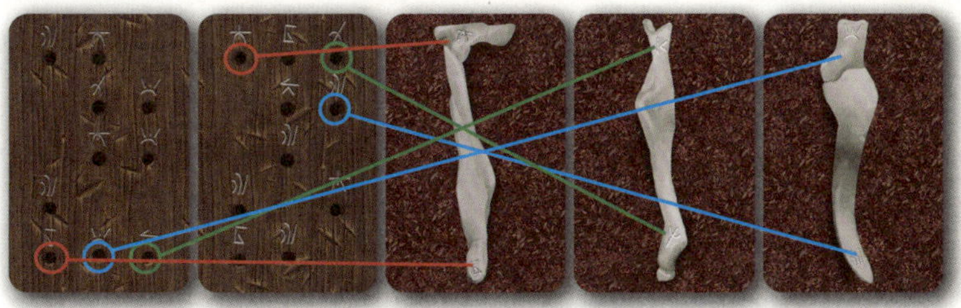

Once the heroes have found the solution, the GM reads the following aloud.

"You manage to escape without getting noticed by the gorillas. As you leave, you get your hands on a curious wooden chest, which Brann Bronzebeard certainly wanted to put in a safe place, but the gorillas have forced open. Inside, you discover a new crystal and some old papers."

GM: Give the heroes cards 48 and 50.
Read the following as you present card 45.

"You pick up the pace and see the west lake on the horizon. After walking for what feels like an eternity, the ground suddenly starts shaking violently. A stone guardian bursts up from the ground, cutting a chasm into the earth that splits your group and blocks your path! The churning earth and stone fill the air with a cacophony, making it impossible to hear your fellow adventurers."

GM: Divide the heroes in two teams.
Give one team card 51 and give the other card 52.
Read the following to the heroes.

"The papers you just discovered were torn in the commotion. It is too dangerous to try and pass the stone guardian without a plan. Now that your party is split up, you can only use cards in your area. Heroes within the same group can share their cards or documents with each other but not the other group. To communicate with each other, the heroes have to act out (charades) their information for the other group to interpret."

PUZZLE 9: VICTORY CRYSTALLIZED

CARDS: 45, 46, 47, 48, 49, 50, 51, and 52

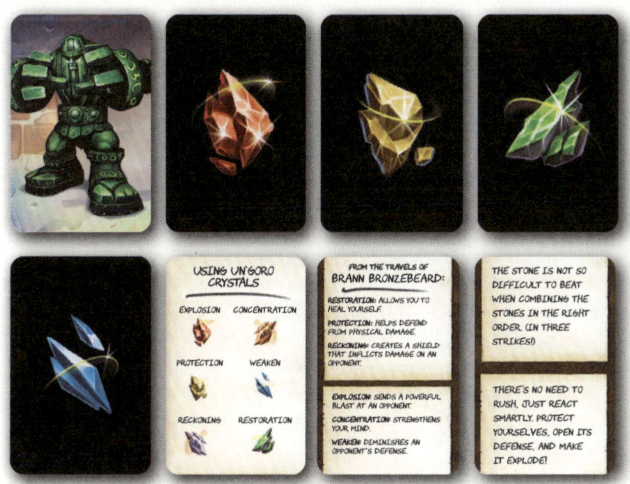

If the heroes already have found all the elements needed to solve this puzzle, distribute the resources equally between the two teams. If not, the players must continue to search their respective areas and cannot show the other team what cards they find. They can talk amongst their group, but must act out the information to the other group.

GM: Read the following aloud.

"You have neither the weapons nor the numbers to fight this stone guardian. You must find another way to vanquish this powerful enemy."

When the players understand how they must use the crystals, the GM tells them that the fight is about to begin. Each time the heroes make mistakes in the order of the combinations, the GM reads the following aloud.

"The combination didn't work. The crystals spark and fizzle, but no effect is produced. It will take 30 seconds for the crystals to recover."

The players have to wait 30 seconds before starting again.

GM CLUES:

1. Some of you have an order; the others have a way. When you cannot hear, movement is your best chance.

2. You can combine the crystals to defeat the guardian, but you must do it correctly.

3. Brann Bronzebeard went through those dangers many times before you. His advice is precious. And sometimes, literal.

METHOD:

Thanks to the words of Brann Bronzebeard, the heroes understand they have to combine three crystals to destroy the stone guardian. Group B knows they have to protect themselves, open the stone guardian's defenses, and make the stone guardian explode. Group A knows what each crystal does. They know that "Protection" allows them to defend themselves, that "Weaken" diminishes an opponent's defense, and that "Explosion" sends a powerful blast at an opponent. By communicating they can understand the order of the combination: PROTECTION – WEAKEN – EXPLOSION.

SOLUTION:

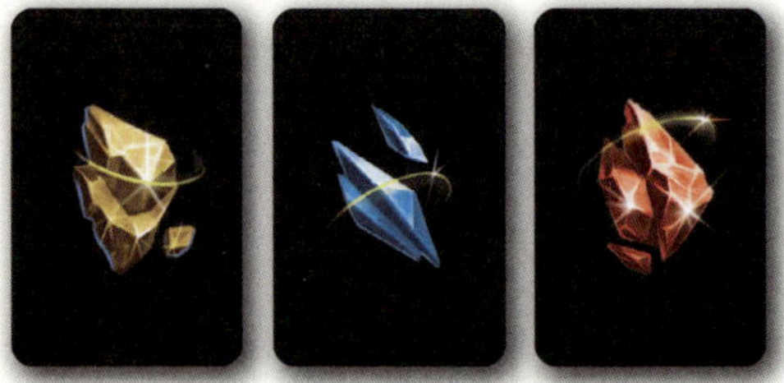

The heroes must use "Protection" (card 47), then "Weaken" (card 49), and finally "Explosion" (card 46).

Once the heroes have found the solution, the GM reads the following:

> *"The explosion crystal creates a blast that reduces the stone guardian to rubble. The wreckage of the guardian fills the chasm, allowing the separated party members to cross safely. Behind you, you can hear the wild cries of the terrible creatures of Un'Goro.*

When you round the west lake and reach the top of the crater, you take one last look at the gigantic branches. With a sigh of relief, you return to the white desert of Tanaris that stretches out under a starry sky. You and your team got each other through primordial perils, and Brann Bronzebeard's guidance kept you safe.

Congratulations! You have survived the many dangers of Un'Goro Crater!"

PUTRICIDE'S LABORATORY OF HORRORS

DIFFICULTY 🟢🟢⚪

You find yourselves prisoner in the laboratory of the terrible Professor Putricide. Here, hideous things ooze with vile, purulent slime—and you will soon join them. He's planning to test his new plague of undeath on your party. Will you escape before your blood runs cold?

PROFESSOR PUTRICIDE

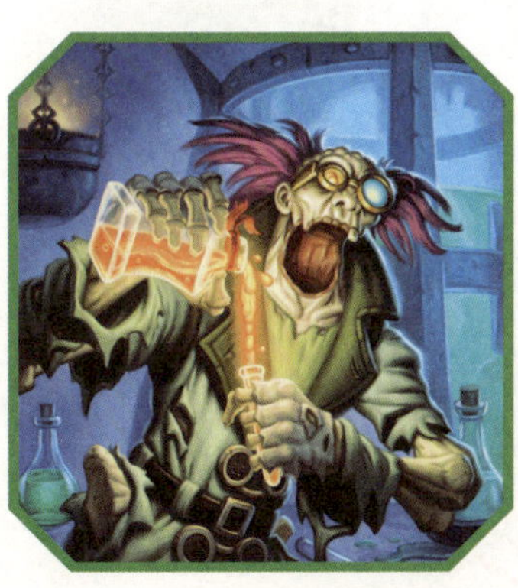

Good news, everyone! During the game, Professor Putricide will speak, and the Game Master will be the actor playing him. To bring Putricide to life, feel free to use a slightly higher-pitched, raspy voice for his narration—but above all, a passionate one! You are proud of your plague and can't wait to see its effects.

UNIQUE RULE: THE PLAGUE OF UNDEATH

After the second puzzle is solved, the Game Master (GM) will announce to the heroes that Putricide's experiment has already begun and that **one of them is turning undead**.

Alongside the 60 minutes of the soundtrack, you must start a **5-minute Spread the Plague countdown**. If this countdown reaches 0, the plague spreads and an additional player is infected.

The game is lost if all players become undead.

To prevent the countdown from reaching 0, the heroes must find Temporary Serum cards by solving puzzles or by searching the play area. These cards include extra time (5, 10, or 15 minutes) to delay the spread of the plague. When such a card is discovered, add the time it indicates to the countdown.

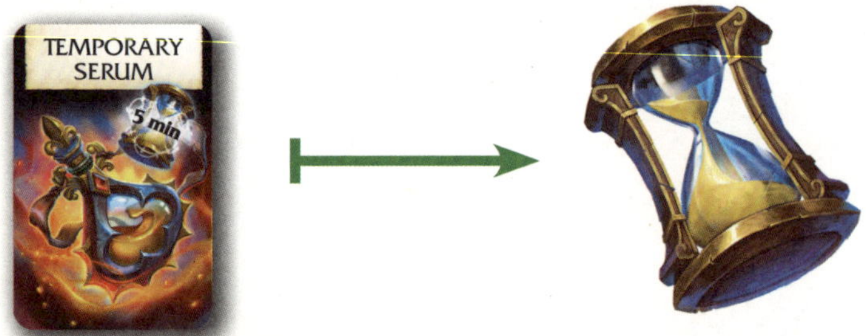

The heroes discover a 5-minute Temporary Serum card.

The Game Master adds five minutes to the Spread timer.

THE COUNTDOWN REACHES 0: WHAT DO YOU DO?

The last player touched by an infected player is in turn infected with the Plague of Undeath. Inform the newly infected player, then add 5 minutes to the countdown and continue the adventure.

The number of Temporary Serum cards used for this scenario may be varied according to the number of heroes.

	2 HEROES	3–4 HEROES	5 HEROES
15 MINUTE	One 15-minute card kept in the GM's hand		
10 MINUTE	One 10-minute card kept in the GM's hand	Two 10-minute cards kept in the GM's hand	One 10-minute card kept in the GM's hand
5 MINUTE	Five 5-minute cards, two kept by the GM and three hidden in the game area	Six 5-minute cards, three kept by the GM and three hidden in the game area.	Eight 5-minute cards, four kept by the GM and four hidden in the game area

NOTE: The Temporary Serum cards are not numbered.

If desired, the GM can decide how many Temporary Serum cards to use. What matters is that the total time on the cards adds up to at least 50 minutes.

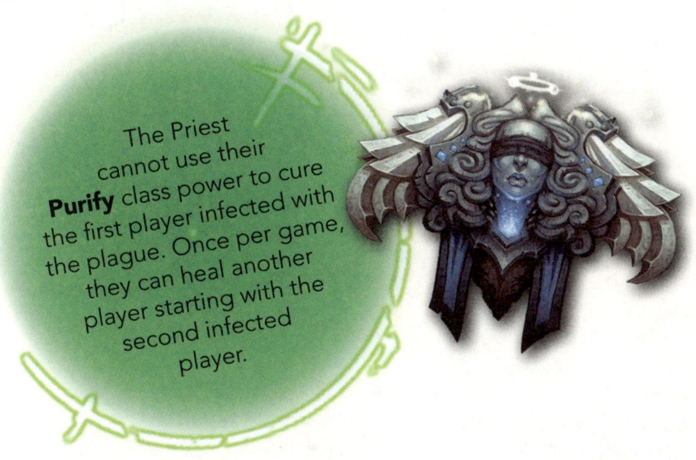

SCENARIO EVENTS

Scenario events allow the GM to vary the difficulty of this scenario and add more role-playing flavor. The GM is free to trigger events whenever they like or not at all.

Miasma Leak: The affected player has breathed in a harmful substance. They cannot talk for 5 minutes. They can still write and gesture.

Side Effects: Heroes affected by the plague are prone to side effects. Now stricken with fatigue, they can only move by crawling on their knees for 5 minutes. If the players cannot or do not want to crawl, they can move in slow motion for 5 minutes.

Proximity: Because of how close together the players are in the lab, the plague spreads faster than expected. By triggering this event, another hero is immediately infected. *This event cannot be used if there is only one player left to infect.*

Uncontrolled Explosion: By touching and fiddling with everything in the lab, the heroes end up causing an explosion. The designated player can use only one of their arms for 5 minutes. The priest can use their power to cure the affected player.

SETTING UP THE SCENARIO

This scenario uses cards 1 to 35 and the "Formula" document.

LEAVE THESE CARDS VISIBLE	GM KEEPS THESE CARDS IN THEIR HANDS	HIDE THESE CARDS	HIDE THESE CARDS IN CHALLENGING PLACES
1, 2, 3, 4, 5; "Formula" document.	6, 11, 15, 20, 21, 24, 28, 29, 30, 32, 34, 35	7, 8, 9, 12, 16, 17, 22, 27, 31	10, 13, 14, 18, 19, 23, 25, 26, 33

In total, there are 18 cards to hide, 5 to leave visible, and 12 to keep in your hand. This total excludes the 11 Temporary Serum cards, some of which may stay in the GM's hand or be hidden throughout the game space.

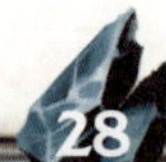

Once you have finished setting up, bring the heroes into the game space. Have them sit in various places in the room, hands behind their backs, and ask them to close their eyes. Make sure they can see the cards you left visible when they open their eyes.

Create a subdued atmosphere if possible. Get creative and decorate if you are feeling ambitious! Scan the included QR code to acquire the accompanying scenario soundtrack.

INTRODUCTION

GM: Read this to players before starting the game.

"Your eyes are closed. Gradually, a pungent scent pulls you out of the mists of unconsiousness: rotting flesh."

GM: Ask the players to open their eyes.

"As you attempt to move, you realize that you are bound by heavy metal chains. You strain against the irons, but your head starts to swim as you struggle.

A strange greenish mist stings your nostrils, making some of you cough. Through the vapors, you spot a set of surgical tools and vials filled with substances that you shudder to even think about. Old bones eagerly gnawed upon by huge rats are piled up in corners of the room— the whole scene sends a shiver down your spine.

A voice echoes aloud and makes you all bolt upright:

'Welcome! I am Professor Putricide and you, my friends, are in for a killer time! I've come up with a whole new formula for my Plague of Undeath. Being vital is such a bore. Don't you want to amble, shamble, and scramble about as the unliving do? Well, you're going to soon! The best part about my new formula is… that I'll be testing it out on you! Hahahaha!'

The voice fades. You look around at one another: members of the Horde and the Alliance who, under any other circumstances, would already be at each other's throats. In this gloomy place, though, your differences are the least of your worries. You must get out of here before Putricide makes lifeless husks of all of you!

Fortunately, one of you manages to wriggle out of your chains. Perhaps your stamina was less depleted."

GM: Tell a hero of your choice that they have managed to free themselves. They are the only person who can move around the room. With five heroes playing, you can free two heroes.

"You must find a way to free the others!"

GM: Start the soundtrack for this scenario.

PUZZLE 1: DISSOLVE THE CHAINS

CARDS: 1, 2, 3, 4, 5, and the "Formula" Document

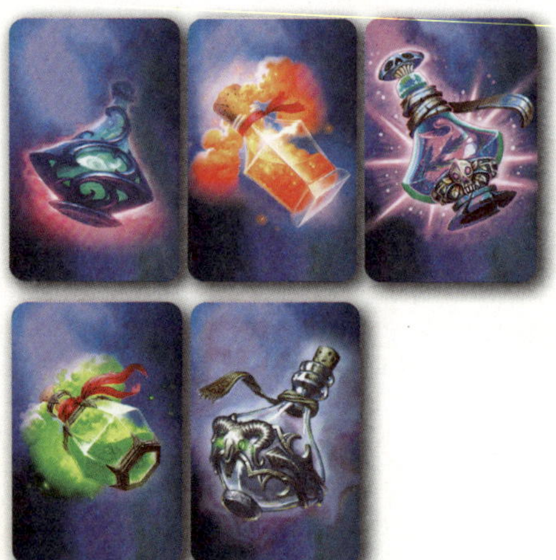

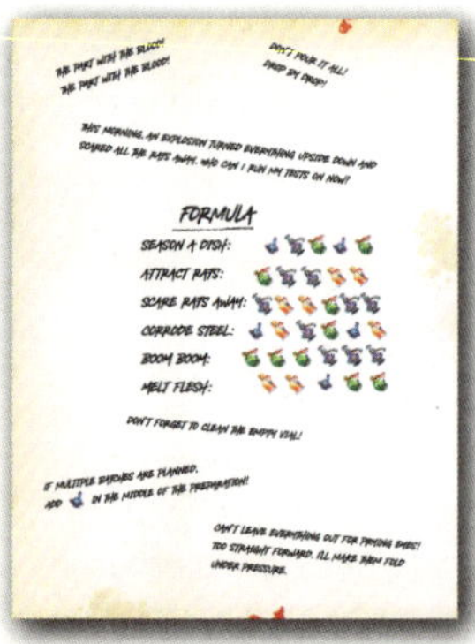

FORMULA

SEASON A DISH:

ATTRACT RATS:

SCARE RATS AWAY:

CORRODE STEEL:

BOOM BOOM:

MELT FLESH:

"FORMULA" DOCUMENT

GM CLUES:

1. The correct formulas have been obscured. You'll need to remove some of the vials!

2. You need an empty vial to make the mixture.

3. Have you thought of folding the document by following Putricide's notes?

METHOD:

Once the four vials and the empty vial have been noted, the heroes must choose the right formula: "**Corrode steel.**"

The formulas have been obscured, so the heroes must follow the various instructions written down by Putricide: Fold the document along a line that joins the two blood stains, and add a drop from the blue vial before the one from the yellow vial.

SOLUTION:

The heroes must tell you the following mix:

CORRODE STEEL: 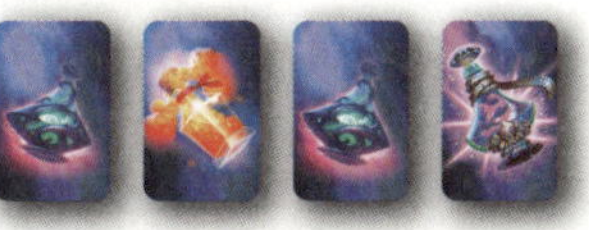

When they do so, read them the following text:

> *"In a matter of seconds, the corrosive mixture melts through the chains that had held you prisoner. You are now all free to move. You discover a strange chest and a door locked by a ghastly bone mechanism. There's no other way out, so you'll need to figure out how to open them."*

GM: Give the heroes cards 6 and 11.

PUZZLE 2: THE OLD CHEST

CARDS: 11, 12, 13, and 14

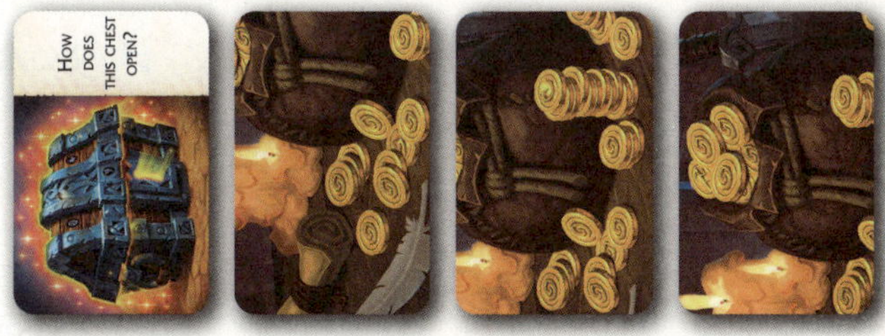

GM CLUES:

1. Each coin has more than one detail.
2. Have you considered looking at the coins from a different angle?

METHOD:

The heroes need to look carefully at the coins and the mechanism to find what they have in common.

This common feature is found on the face of the coins and in the recesses in the front of the chest.

SOLUTION:

The heroes must tell you which coin they want to use and where.

The solution is therefore: Left indentation — Coin on card 13

Center indentation — Coin on card 12

Right indentation — Coin on card 14

If they are wrong, you can apply the **Uncontrolled Explosion** event.

When they find the solution, read them the following text:

"The old chest opens with a grim creak. Inside, you find a temporary serum, an electronic lever, and an old note document."

GM: Give the heroes cards 20 and 32, as well as the Temporary Serum card with the most time that you have kept in your hand.

PUZZLE 3: BITE

CARDS: 6, 7, 8, 9, and 10

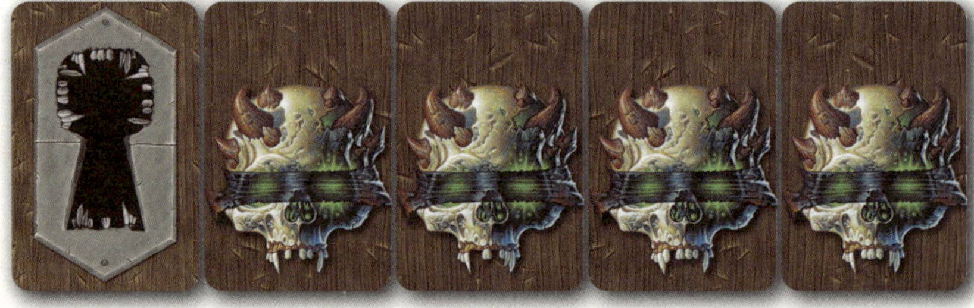

GM CLUES:

1. Those notches aren't there by accident. They have an interesting pattern.
2. What if they worked like the pins of a lock?

METHOD:

Once the heroes have the four skulls in their possession, they must place them correctly on the mechanism. Each skull's **teeth must align with the notches** on one side of the mechanism.

SOLUTION:

The heroes must correctly place the skulls on the device.

When they do so, read them the following text:

"The strange door opens. You make your way down a grimy ladder and discover a lab filled with all kinds of tools and contraptions. In one corner of the room, you see a severed abomination head that Putricide probably used for one of his experiments."

GM: Give the heroes card 15.

"You hear Putricide's voice again:

'Not so fast, my little rats! The experiment for my new plague has already begun! Why do you think one of you was able to break free so easily? Their body has already begun to wither and decay.'

GM: Tell the first hero who was able to move freely that they are carrying the plague.
Then give all the heroes the following information:

*"You face a new threat: **the Plague of Undeath**. It will spread among you. I will start a **5-minute countdown**. Alongside the puzzles, you must find **Temporary Serum** cards that will add time to this countdown and prevent the spread of the plague.*

If the countdown reaches 0, another hero will be infected.

You lose if all heroes become infected.

If there is a Priest among you, their power can cure one player of the infection (except for the first infected player)."

Ask the heroes if they have any questions; otherwise, ask them to continue looking for a way to leave this place (and resume the soundtrack).

PUZZLE 4: IT'S ALIVE!

CARDS: 15, 16, 17, 18, 19, and 20

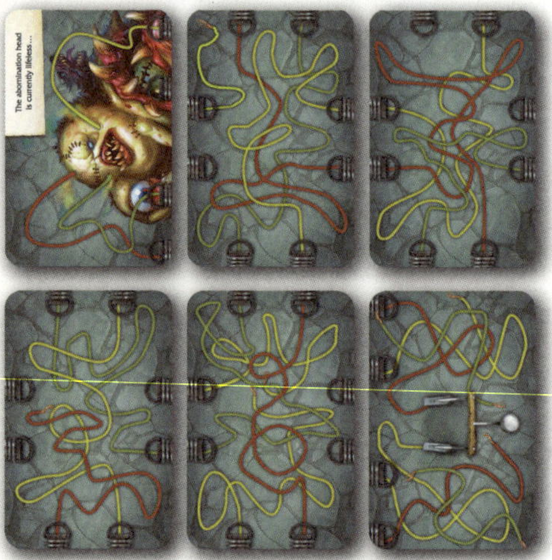

GM CLUES:

1 Carefully observe the wires that start from the lever or head.

2 There are three different types of wires. You may not need all three.

METHOD: The heroes must correctly place cards 15-19 to form a direct path between the yellow and orange wires that connect the head and the control switch.

SOLUTION:

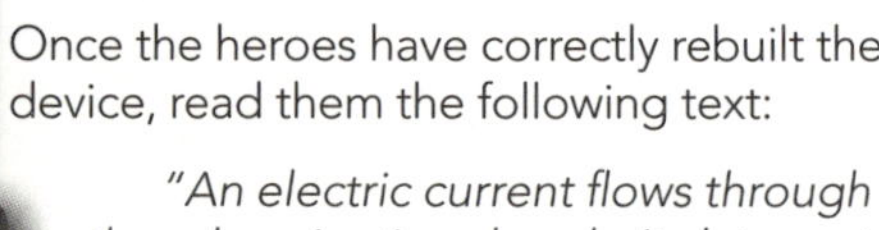

Once the heroes have correctly rebuilt the device, read them the following text:

"An electric current flows through the abomination head. It lets out a horrifying gasp, then spits out a piece of paper."

GM: Give the heroes card 21.

"The head then starts mumbling. You ask it how to get out of here.

'Password! Paaaasswooooorrrrrd! Else not say nothing. And you get out, get out!'

The abomination head seems to be waiting for a password."

PUZZLE 5: PASSWORD

CARDS: 21, 22, and 23

GM CLUES:

1 Putricide's words on this paper seem innocuous enough. What if he hid something in them?

2 A password should be easy to remember. And sometimes, not even a real word.

3 What if these numbers indicated locations?

METHOD: The text of card 21 outlines what to do: "through these lines, words, and letters." "LWL" means **Line, Word, Letter.** The numbers on cards 22 and 23 indicate where the letters are.

Card 22 gives "PUTRE" and card 23 gives "STINK." The heroes just need to reconstruct the password to get the solution.

SOLUTION: The heroes must find the word "**PUTRESTINK**."

Once they have done it, read them the following text:

> *"The head flails around, thick greenish phlegm dripping from its mouth as it speaks.*
>
> *'Pu . . . Putre . . . Putrestink!' it says. 'Hahaha! He sure does stink! Password good!'*
>
> *With great effort, the head then brokenly explains to you that the only way to get past Putricide and out of the lab safely is with a teleportation stone. But you still have to get your hands on it . . .*
>
> *The head tells you about an encoder hidden in the room as well.*
>
> *You also find a vial of temporary serum."*

GM: Give the heroes card 24 and a 5-minute Temporary Serum card.

PUZZLE 6: THE ENCODER

CARDS: 24, 25, and 26

GM CLUES:

1. The order in which Putricide activated the letters on the encoder is visible.

2. The code has changed since it was last used.

3. Some things are written in reverse, but you do not have to reverse everything.

4. There is a link between the square impressions on the encoder and the arrows, but what is it?

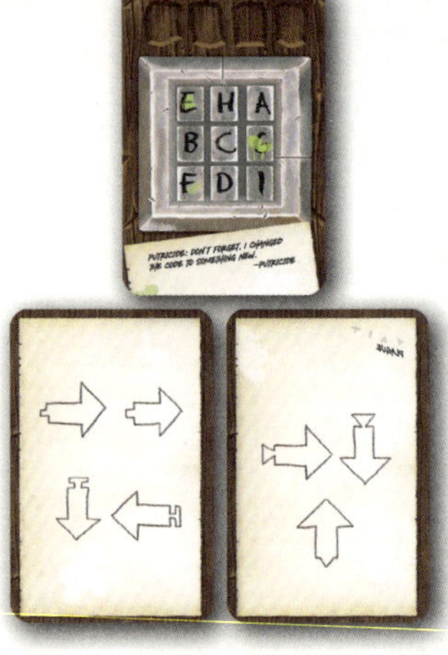

METHOD: The heroes find the last code Putricide typed in—**G E F C**—by following the fingerprints on the encoder. They can see that, as he typed, Putricide's finger had less and less substance on it.

The heroes must then make the connection between the indentations above the encoder and the arrows on cards 25 and 26. Thus, the first square with the inverted triangle on top refers to the arrows with inverted triangles on card 26. Following the clue to reverse the instructions on card 26, the G becomes a H; and the E becomes a B. Card 25 does not show a reversal clue, so the F becomes an I and the C becomes an F.

SOLUTION: The heroes must find the code **H B I F**.

If they are wrong, the GM can apply the **Miasma Leak** event.

Once they have found the solution, the GM reads the following aloud:

> *"Now that the correct code has been entered, a recess appears in one of the walls. Inside is a teleportation stone. Unfortunately, it is disenchanted."*

> GM: Give the heroes card 30, then continue.

> *"The abomination head hums an off-key tune:*
> *'You must… enchant stone!'*
> *As you search the recess, you find a torn-out textbook page and a glass vial. As you reach for the pages, the glass topples over and shatters on the floor.*

A thick plume of purple gas rises from the broken bottle and wafts toward you. One of your party members stumbles a bit too close and grazes the vapors with their hand. The skin immediately rots and turns to ash. There is no way you can push through the gas and survive. There must be a way to neutralize the gas."

GM: Give the heroes card 28.

PUZZLE 7: STUDY WELL

CARDS: 27 and 28

GM CLUES:

1 This seems to be the third volume of the text book.

2 This is a laboratory with many reagents and ingredients stored within. If you can figure out what you need to make, you should be able to make it.

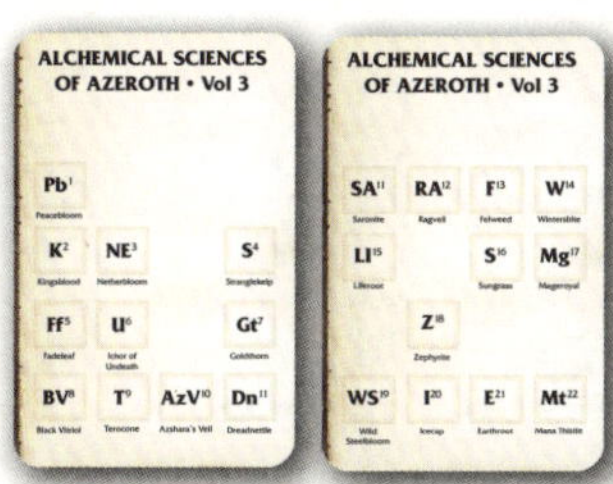

METHOD:

Select the components whose numbers are all multiples of three (in sequence) Netherbloom, Ichor of Undeath, Terocone, Ragveil, Liferoot, Zephyrite, and Earthroot.

The component abbreviations will spell the word **NEUTRALIZE**.

SOLUTION:

Spelling the word will confirm the correct solution.

If they submit an incorrect solution, the GM can apply the **Proximity** event once (only if there is more than one player left who is not infected by the Plague of Undeath).

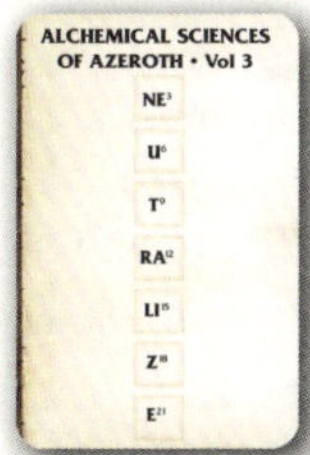

GM: Once the heroes have found the solution, give them card 29 and the Temporary Serum card with the most time left in the GM's hand.

PUZZLE 8: THE FORMULA

CARDS: 30, 31, 32, and 33

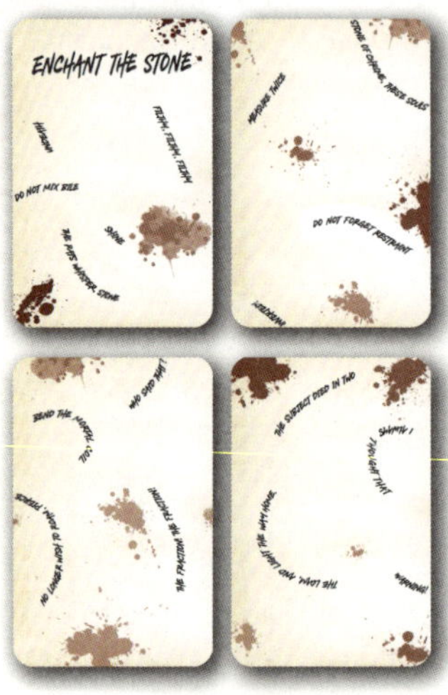

GM CLUE:

1 These pages are filthy—there are stains on every page!

METHOD: The heroes must correctly arrange the four pieces of paper using the stains.

They then will see a sentence appear that allows them to enchant the stone.

SOLUTION: Heroes must say out loud the sentence **"Shine, stone of chrome, these souls no longer wish to roam, pierce the loam, and light the way home."**

GM: Once the heroes have solved the puzzle, give them a 5-minute Temporary Serum card. Then read:

"The teleportation stone starts shining brighter and brighter. You are all about to teleport when the abomination head behind you begins to taunt you in a sing-song voice.

'Run outside, quick! Spr-spread the Plague of Undeath!'

'That's enough!' Putricide's voice bellows from beyond. 'You keep quiet!'

You suddenly understand. It was all too simple. Your escape was part of Putricide's plan, so that you would spread the Plague across Azeroth.

Disobediently, the head goes on:

'You've… had all you need… this whole time… to cure!'

You absolutely must find a way to cure yourselves before you leave the lab!"

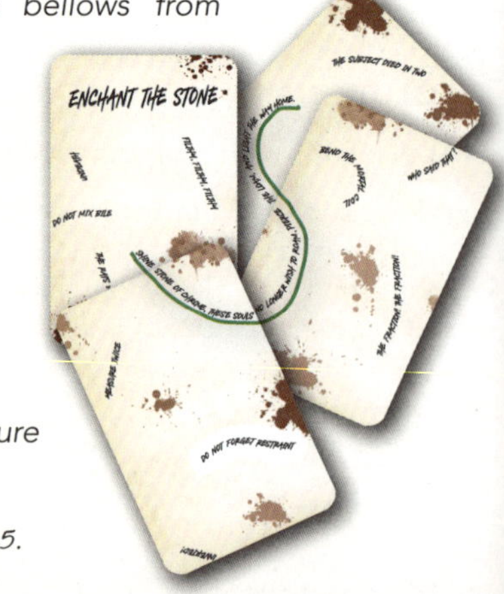

GM: Give the heroes cards 34 and 35.

PUZZLE 9: THE CURE

CARDS: 3, 10, 22, 28, 34, and 35

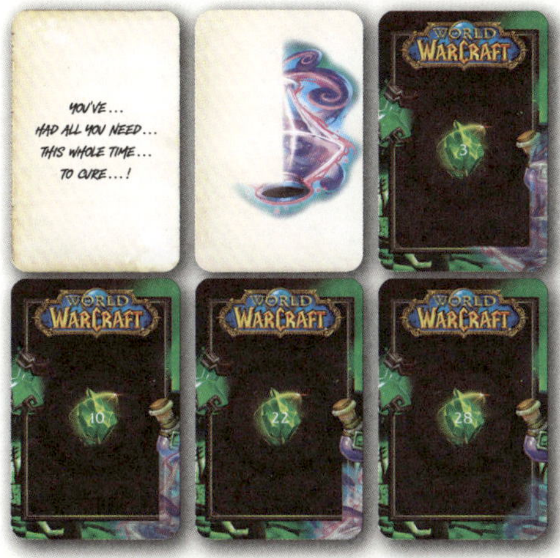

GM CLUES:

1 Don't forget to look at everything you've had in your hands.

2 Behind, perhaps?

3 One part on top of another can make a whole.

METHOD: Based on the words of the abomination head, the heroes understand that the solution to this puzzle can be found on the back of some of the cards.

With card backs 3, 10, 22, and 28, the heroes complete the vial on card 35.

SOLUTION:

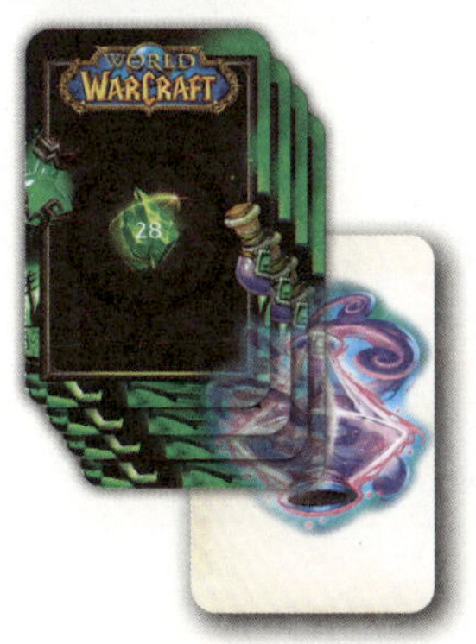

When the heroes show the solution, stop the soundtrack and read the following aloud:

"Each of you drinks part of the potion. The effects of the Plague of Undeath disappear. You are cured!

Putricide's voice erupts from the halls.

'What? How? How did you do that?! NOOOOOO!'

You all gather around the teleportation stone as the abomination head bursts out in great peals of laughter, then starts to hum a tune. Infuriated, Putricide yells at it.

You all teleport together and find yourselves outside. Fresh, crisp air fills your lungs. You don't waste any time, rushing off with your feet sinking into the thick snow. You are free of Professor Putricide's wretched laboratory and back in the world of the living."

TIME UNRELENTING IN KARAZHAN

Rumors surrounding the mysterious tower of Karazhan are circulating once again. Intrigued, a party of heroes from the Horde and the Alliance set out to put these rumors—and their cause—to rest. Narrowly escaping a magical explosion, you now find yourselves trapped inside the tower only to discover that the passage of time within has become unstable. Will you manage to solve Karazhan's many mysteries and prevent your reality from collapsing?

SCENARIO EVENTS

The below events allow the Game Master (GM) to vary the difficulty of this scenario. The GM is free to trigger these events whenever they like.

Time Shift: The designated player is not aligned with the same flow of time as the others. They cannot talk and can only use gestures for 5 minutes.

Arcane Annihilation: The designated player has been exposed to arcane magic for too long. Partially paralyzed by this powerful energy, they can no longer touch any cards with their hands. (Creative workarounds are acceptable.)

Ghost from the Past: The designated player experiences curious visions. For 5 minutes, they can only communicate with the other heroes by drawing. (They are not allowed to write words.)

The Truth is Out There: The designated player is affected by time being mixed up: part of their mind is trapped in another temporality. For the next 5 minutes, they are forced to lie to the other heroes.

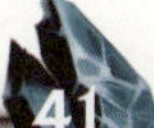

SETTING UP THE SCENARIO

This scenario uses cards 1 to 41, the poster, the prism, and the Apprentice's Notebook.

GM KEEPS THESE CARDS IN THEIR HANDS	HIDE THESE CARDS	HIDE THESE CARDS IN CHALLENGING PLACES
1, 8, 14, 15, 16, 20, 24, 25, 26, 27, 29, 30, 31, 32, 33, 34, 35, 36, 37, 38, 39, 40, 41; Apprentice's Notebook; poster; prism	2, 3, 4, 9, 10, 13, 17, 21, 28	5, 6, 7, 11, 12, 18, 19, 22, 23

In total, there are 18 cards to hide, and 23 cards to keep in your hand.
The GM must prepare the prism in advance by cutting out the object and folding it along the lines indicated. If needed, tape the edges together.

Once the setup is complete, the Game Master may ask the players to enter the game space. Scan the included QR code to acquire the accompanying scenario soundtrack.

INTRODUCTION

GM: Read the following to players before starting the game.

"The wind wails between the twisted, leafless trees like a harrowing cry. Your combined force of Horde and Alliance heroes is heading through Deadwind Pass and approaching the dark tower of Karazhan.

In the years since the Last Guardian Medivh vanished, rumors about the old tower have been plentiful but never credible. That is, until now.

'Huge explosions, I tell you!' A frightened informant had told your group through chattering teeth. 'I was on my way to the Swamp of Sorrows when I heard one go off. I couldn't help but go see. At first, I thought Karazhan was ablaze. The next moment, it suddenly looked as splendid as it did before the First War. Then there was another explosion.'

Stories like theirs grew in number. As honorable champions of the Horde and the Alliance, you have agreed to set your differences aside and make sure that no evil is growing in Karazhan.

The tower finally appears, its dilapidated pinnacle piercing the mist. It is deserted and locked shut. Silent. Suddenly, the tense crackle of magic fills the air. An explosion upheaves the ground beneath you and shakes stones from the tower above. As you are about to be crushed, the once-locked doors of Karazhan burst open. Cold hands cover your nose and mouth and swiftly pull you inside. In response, the magic grows more aggressive, snapping the doors shut and covering them in a protective aura. A musty odor fills your nostrils. You find yourself inside Karazhan, in a circular room. A shimmering ghost appears beneath a stone archway.

'Help, champions! I am all that is left of Moroes. I was once the steward of this tower. Now, Karazhan is about to be destroyed from the inside out! The magic of this place has gone terribly awry. The past, present, and hereafter are mixing disastrously. Our time is short and Karazhan is filled with traps. In the years before, there were so many aspiring apprentices showing up at the gates of Karazhan that my master, Medivh, devised a series of three challenges to discourage them. You'll need to pass these challenges before you can do anything about Time. . . or the tower will take you down with it. I found this notebook with the remains of one of the unfortunate souls who failed the challenges. Perhaps it will help you more than them.'"

GM: Give the heroes the Apprentice's Notebook and card 1. Begin playing the soundtrack for this scenario, then read the following aloud to the players.

"As you look around the room, there appears to be a neglected platform for a teleportation portal."

PUZZLE 1: THE GUARDIAN'S FIRST CHALLENGE— TRACING RUNES

CARDS: 1, 2, 3, 4, 5, 6, 7; pages 2, 3, and 5 of the Apprentice's Notebook

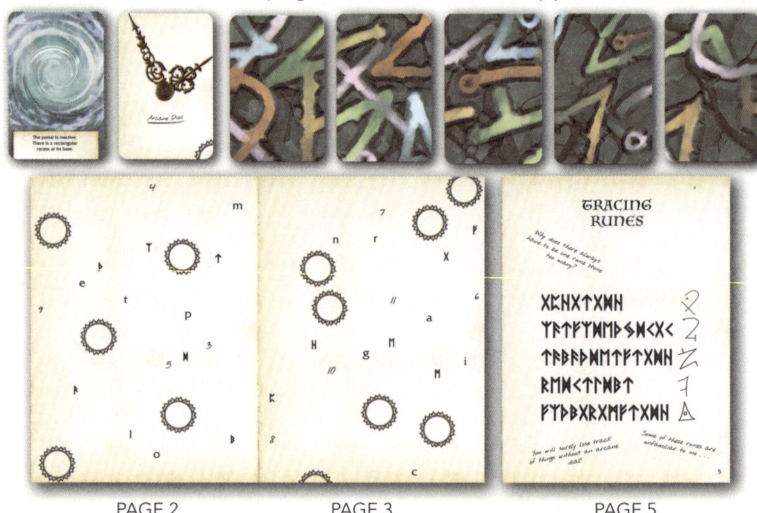

PAGE 2   PAGE 3   PAGE 5

GM CLUES:

1. The first step is translation. You need to find the right tool for this.

2. The arcane dial can be used to translate the encrypted alphabet, but you must place it correctly.

3. Once you've identified the teleportation symbol, you'll need to find a way to reproduce it.

4. One of the five stones you have is not needed. Not all letters are given.

METHOD:

Once the players find card 2, featuring the two-handed arcane dial, they can align its ornament, at the bottom right of the card, with the ones on pages 2 and 3 of the Apprentice's Notebook. For each ornament, they can translate a letter by rotating the dial.

Not all the letters will be given, so the heroes will have to deduce the missing letters. Once that's done, they will know which rune relates to teleportation. Make sure that the players complete the translation and do not skip ahead to arranging the runestones.

Using the runestones (cards 3, 4, 5, and 7), the heroes can reform the pattern.
Card 6 is not needed.

SOLUTION:

The heroes must arrange the runestones as follows:

When they do so, the GM reads the following
text aloud.

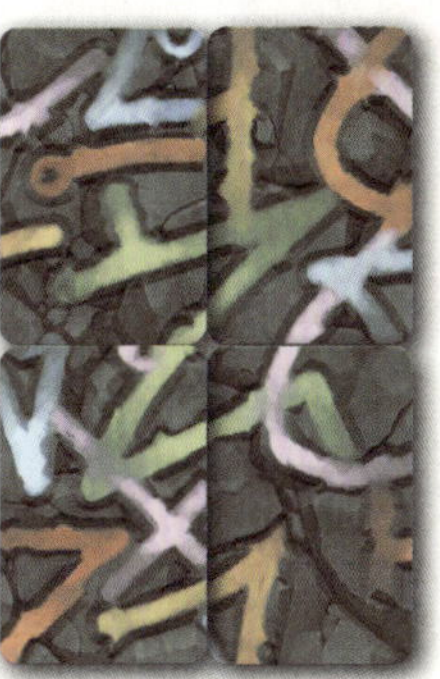

TRANSLATED RUNE NAMES:	KEY		
• IGNITION	ᚠ e	ᛗ o	ᛋ h
• METAMORPHOSIS	ᛗ c	ᛘ r	ᚲ s
• TELEPORTATION	ᛒ l	ᚠ a	ᚱ b
• FROSTBOLT	ᛏ t	ᚷ i	ᚴ g
• AMPLIFICATION	ᚦ p	ᚺ n	ᚱ f
		ᛉ m	

*"With a tremor, the portal activates. You jump through just as
another explosion shakes the tower. You find yourselves in the heart
of a mazelike library, squeezed between gigantic dusty bookcases.*

*Moroes's ghostly form materializes next to you. 'Here is the second
challenge. You must fill this bookcase with books. I think so, anyway.'"*

GM: Give the heroes card 8.

PUZZLE 2: THE GUARDIAN'S SECOND CHALLENGE—SORTING BOOKS

CARDS: 8, 9, 10, 11, 12, and 13; page 7 of the Apprentice's Notebook

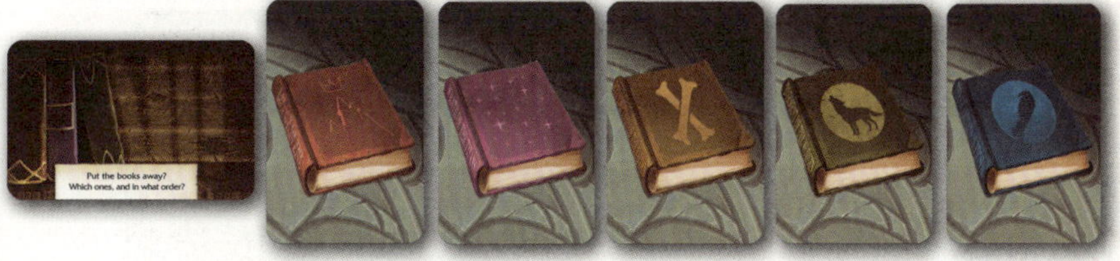

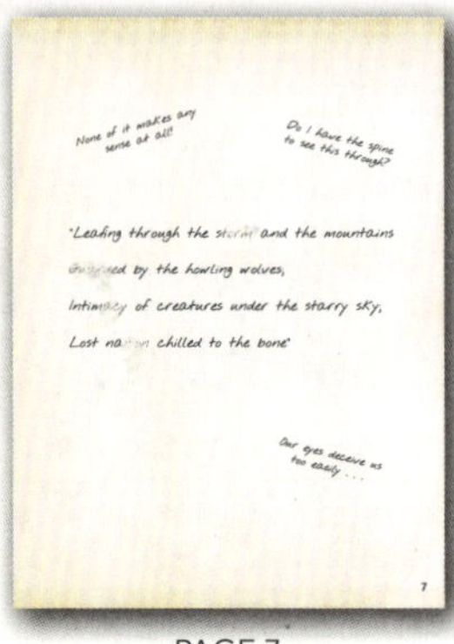

PAGE 7

GM CLUES:

1. Never judge a book by its cover. Have you taken a close look at them?

2. Something is hidden in the words of the poem.

3. One of the books doesn't belong on this shelf.

METHOD:

The heroes begin by finding the five books and identifying that they need to use page 7 of the Apprentice's Notebook.

Once this is done, they notice that some letters in the poem are different from the others.

By carefully looking at the books, and especially their spines, the heroes can read their titles. The smudged letters in the poem match with letters from the titles: "torm" for *Torment of the Worgen*; "guard" for *The Guardians of Tirisfal*; "acy" for *Legacy of the Mountain King*, and "tion" for *Redemption of the Fallen*.

They realize that each line is associated with a book, which gives them the order in which the books are to be placed on the bookcase.

SOLUTION:

The heroes show the GM in what order they will place the books on the bookcase:

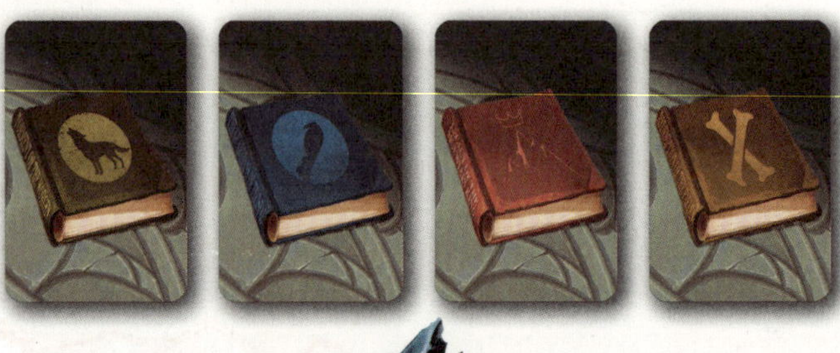

When they do so, the GM reads the following text aloud.

"One of the huge bookcases moves aside to reveal a passage, just as another explosion rattles the hall. The ground begins to shake and buckle.

'Quick!' shouts Moroes. 'Things are getting more and more unstable! You've only got one challenge left!'

You sprint through the passage and enter a dark room. In some places, candles have been placed on strange altars."

GM: Give the heroes cards 14, 15, and 16.

PUZZLE 3: THE GUARDIAN'S THIRD CHALLENGE—THE RITUAL

CARDS: 14, 15, 16, 17, 18, and 19; page 9 of the Apprentice's Notebook

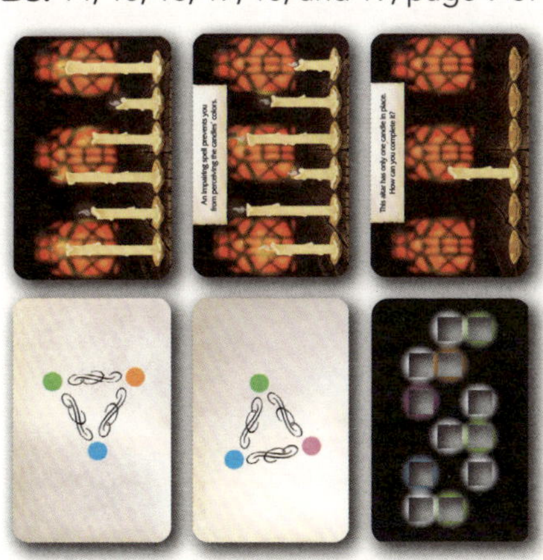

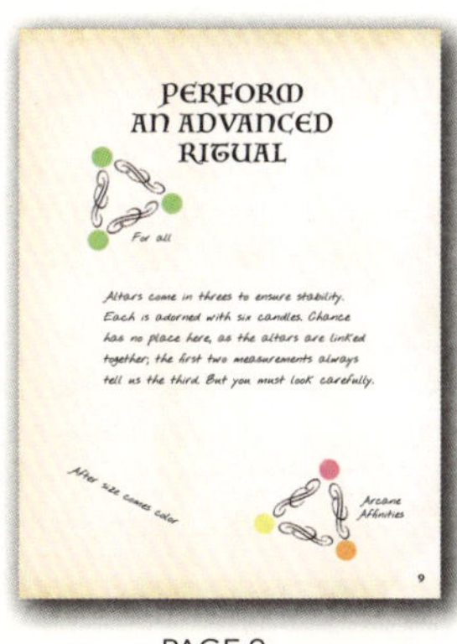

PAGE 9

GM CLUES:

1 What could you possibly "measure"?

2 Start by placing the candles without knowing their colors.

3 Before trying to find the colors for the last ritual, find the ones that are obscured.

4 The affinities will be needed for the final step.

METHOD:

The heroes realize that the three altars are linked, and that they need to find out which candles go in which positions on card 16.

There are three sizes of candles: small, medium, and large. Based on the candle on card 16 and the differently sized candles at the same position on cards 14 and 15, the heroes realize that for each of the six positions, each of the three linked altars must have a different candle size at that position. Using process of elimination, card 16's candle sizes are short, short, medium, short, tall, and medium.

Once the sizes of the different candles have been found, the heroes will examine the Arcane Affinities—but to use them, they must first find the colors of the candles on card 15. They do this using card 19, which, when correctly placed, makes the colored halos of the candles appear. With the other two altars' colors now known, heroes can use the Arcane Affinities to determine card 16's missing colors: blue, green, green, yellow, yellow, and blue.

SOLUTION:

The heroes must tell you the sizes and colors of the missing candles:

When they do so, the GM removes cards 15 and 16 from the game, and gives the heroes cards 30 and 31 instead (which show the solutions to both altars). The GM then reads the following aloud.

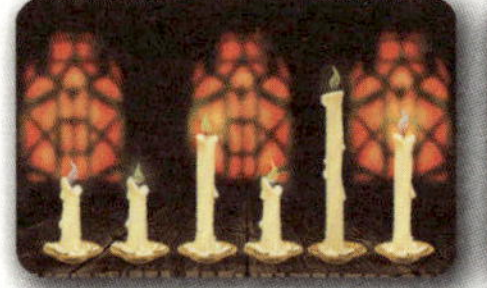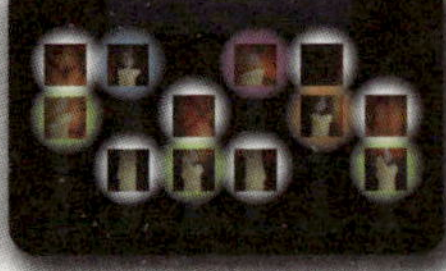

CARD 31, THE SOLUTION TO THE PUZZLE

"The ritual is complete and reveals a magically concealed corridor.

'Incredible!' exclaims Moroes. 'But the time for congratulations will have to wait. Karazhan is pulling a great amount of arcane magic from the ley lines beneath it. We must now climb higher up the tower to reach one of Medivh's inventions, but a spell is blocking the way! You must find a way to dispel it!'"

GM: Give the heroes cards 20, 25, and 27.

PUZZLE 4: THE WALL OF FLAME

CARDS: 20, 21, 22, 23, 25, 27, and 28; page 11 of the Apprentice's Notebook

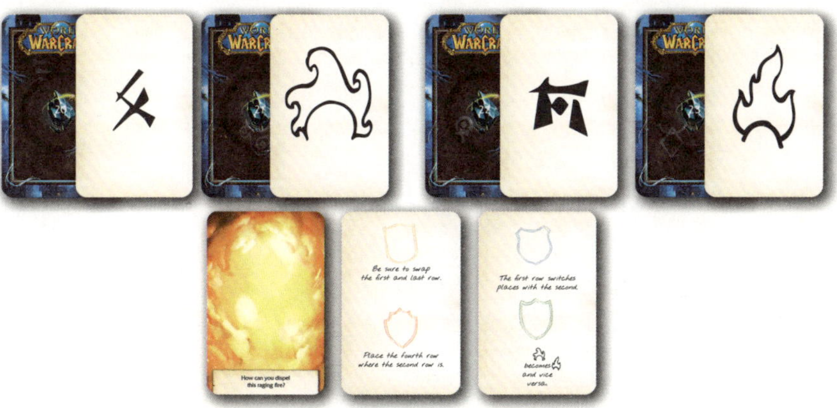

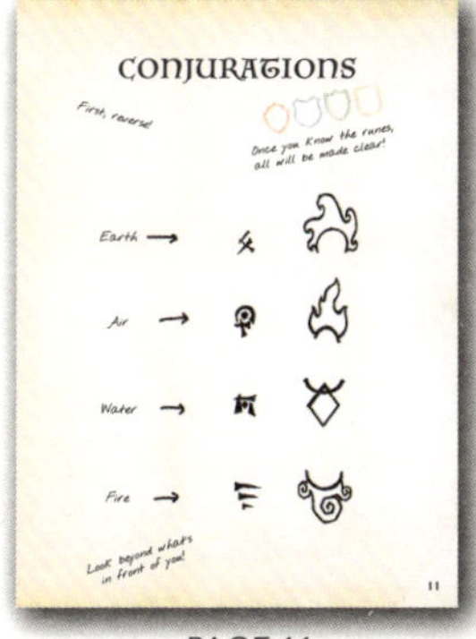

PAGE 11

GM CLUES:

1 Identifying the rune is not enough because all the runes and their parts have been mixed up.

2 To rearrange the runes, you must follow the instructions in the right order.

3 You will need to look closely at all the information you have.

METHOD:

This is an order of operations puzzle. The players will need to follow the instructions on page 11 and cards 27 and 28. The players must examine the fronts and backs of cards 20, 21, 22, and 23 for all the rune pieces they need. Start with "First, reverse!" by swapping all the runes on the card face for their ghosted counterparts on the card backs (and vice versa). Then follow the instructions beside the red, blue, green and finally yellow sigils to reconstruct the runes and match them with the correct element.

SOLUTION:

When the heroes correctly arrange the rune cards, the GM hands them card 26. The heroes must provide the rune that can douse the flames—the water rune. When provided, the GM reads the following aloud.

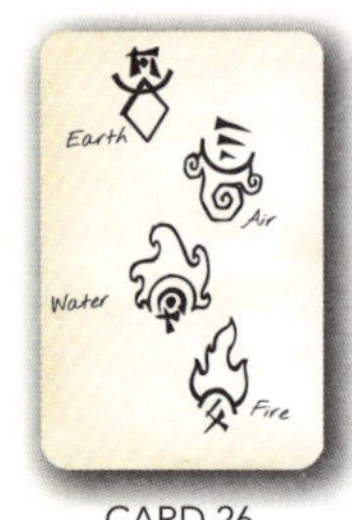

CARD 26

> "The wall of flame disappears. You enter the highest floor of the tower. Arcane explosions ring out from all directions.
>
> 'There it is!' shouts Moroes, pointing to a stand."

GM: Place the poster in the game space, preferably on a table, as well as the prism, and card 29. The GM must prepare the prism in advance.

> "This is one of Medivh's last inventions. The contraption allows the user to control the arcane magic flows that converge within Karazhan. The safeguards set up around this device have fallen—that explains the temporal disturbances. We must stabilize the past, present, and hereafter of Karazhan if we are to succeed."

PUZZLE 5: STABILIZE KARAZHAN—PAST

MATERIALS: Card 29; Poster, Prism, and page 13 of the Apprentice's Notebook

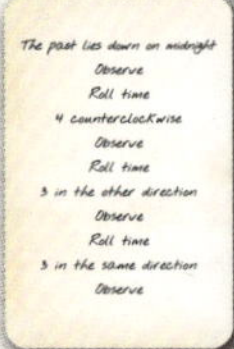

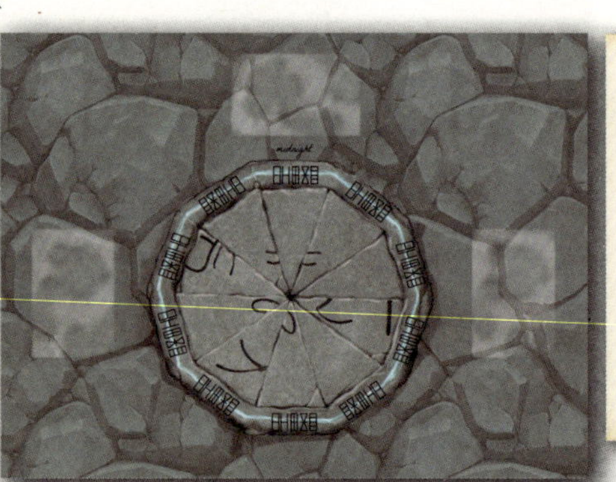

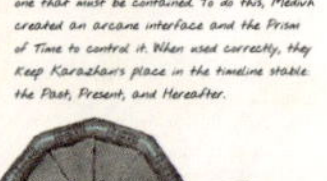

PRISM OF TIME: INSTRUCTIONS FOR USE

Karazhan is an incredible source of magic, but one that must be contained. To do this, Medivh created an arcane interface and the Prism of Time to control it. When used correctly, they keep Karazhan's place in the timeline stable: the Past, Present, and Hereafter.

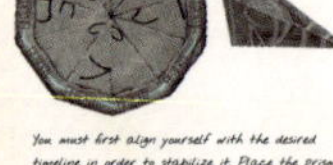

You must first align yourself with the desired timeline in order to stabilize it. Place the prism and follow the instructions. Find the right letter of power to say. You just need to look carefully.

13

PAGE 13

GM CLUES:

1. Does the shape of the Prism remind you of anything related to the panel?
2. Once in place, the Prism takes on a new appearance.
3. Is there anything you can easily roll?

METHOD:

The heroes place the Prism in the direction indicated at the top, at "midnight," with the "past" face laying face-down against the Poster as described on card 29.

They then "roll" the Prism in the direction indicated, one position after another, following the instructions correctly. At each stage, they must observe the panel, because a letter is completed by the prism.

SOLUTION:

The heroes must say the letters "**K O A Z**."

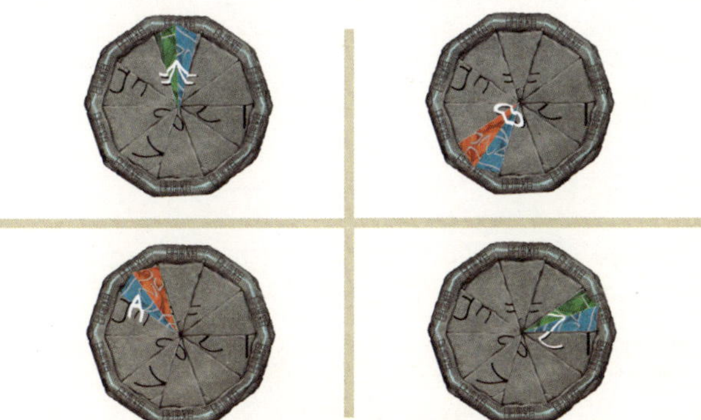

Once the heroes say the word, the GM reads the following text aloud.

> *"The air of the Netherspace thrums and the interface shakes.*
>
> *'Yes!' Moroes says happily. 'The magic is aligned with the past! And look! Something from the past has just appeared!'*
>
> *A strange altar and an engraving appear on the esplanade."*
>
> *GM: Give the heroes cards 32 and 33.*

PUZZLE 6: THE FOURTH ALTAR

CARDS: 14, 19, 30, 31, 32, and 33

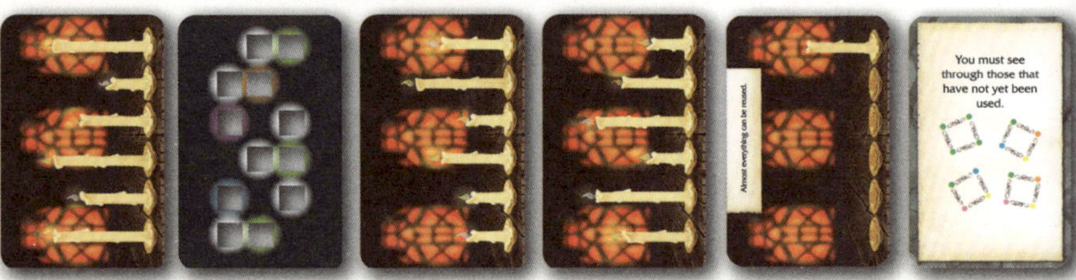

GM CLUES:

1 It makes sense to reuse what you've already used.

2 You've learned the right order for performing one ritual, but there are others out there as well…

3 This time, finding the colors is simple… but how will you determine the sizes of the candles?

4 Looking at the card with the altar, is there a symbol that reminds you of something?

METHOD:

The heroes must use some of the items acquired during Medivh's third challenge, including cards 14, 19, 30, and 31.

As with the previous puzzle, heroes will need to determine the sizes of the candles first. Card 19 is needed for this.

The heroes must correctly place card 19 on top of card 32. Following the instruction "You must see through those that have not yet been used," the heroes will realize that the holes they did not use in the third challenge (with the white halos) determine the sizes of the candles.

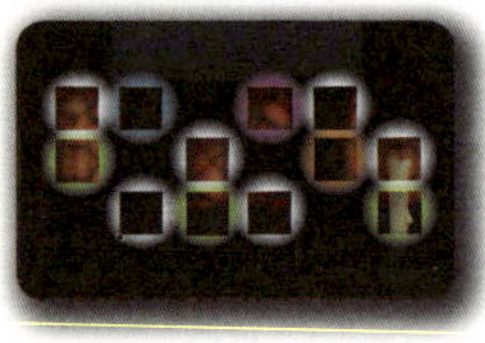

Then all they have to do is find the color of each candle, using card 33 and the Arcane Affinities.

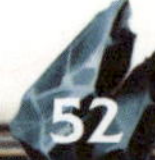

SOLUTION:

The heroes indicate or draw on a document what the altar should look like. The GM then presents the group with the solution on card 24.

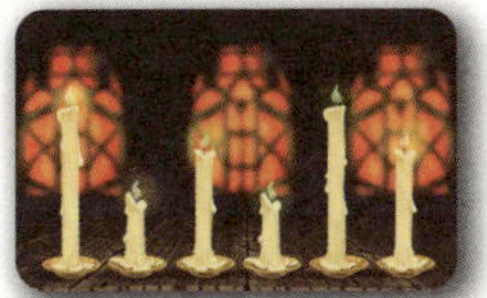

CARD 24, THE SOLUTION TO THE PUZZLE

Once they have found the solution, the GM reads the following aloud.

"'Perfect!' exclaims Moroes. 'Thanks to the ritual, the Past has been stabilized.' A rune appears on the stone panel, locking the magical energies down."

GM: Give the players card 34 and place it on the left box on the Poster.

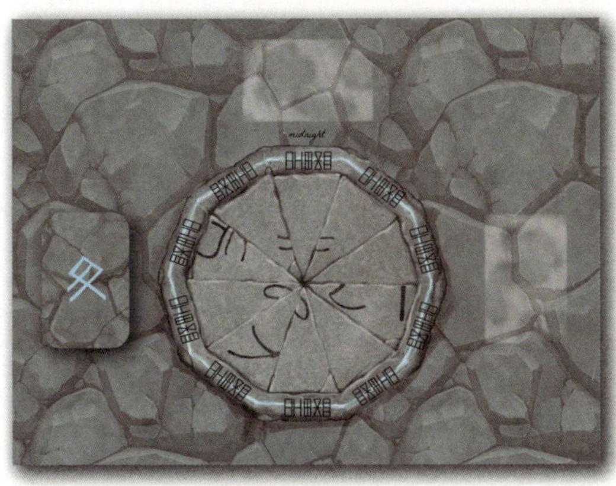

"The rune is in place. Some of the arcane energy is under control! We can't let up now. Onto the hereafter."

GM: Give the heroes card 35.

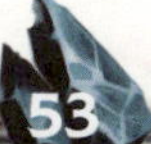

PUZZLE 7: STABILIZE KARAZHAN—HEREAFTER

MATERIALS: Card 35, Poster, and Prism

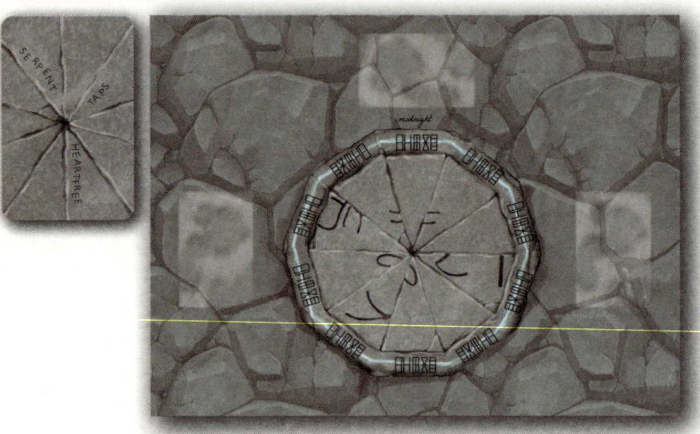

GM CLUES:

1. To find the solution, start by placing the Prism; card 35 is essential.
2. Finding the right order sometimes takes a little disorder.
3. Looking at things head-on is not always enough.

METHOD:

Thanks to card 35, the heroes realize where they will have to place the prism. They will then need to figure out which face to place against the panel.

The heroes realize that the words are anagrams: SERPENT becomes PRESENT, TAPS becomes PAST, HEARTFREE becomes HEREAFTER. As a result, they know which face of the prism must be placed downward, and can discover new letters.

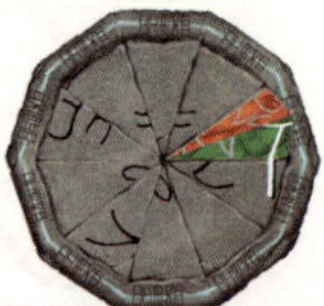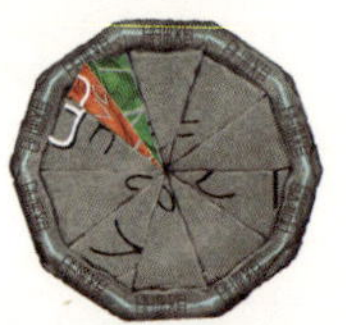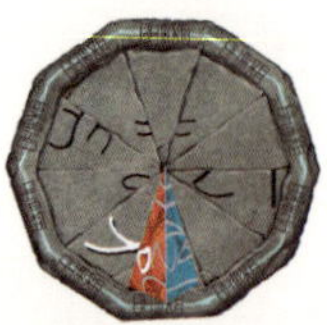

SOLUTION:

The heroes must say the letters **"T E R."**

Once they have found the solution, the GM reads the following text aloud.

"Once again, everything around you shakes.

'The arcane interference is aligned with the hereafter!' Moroes exclaims. 'Present and Hereafter are now overlapping. Wh-What is that?'

Three objects appear before your eyes."

GM: Give the heroes cards 36, 37, and 38.

PUZZLE 8: THE NEW ARCANE DIAL

CARDS: 36, 37, 38; and pages 2 and 3 of the Apprentice's Notebook

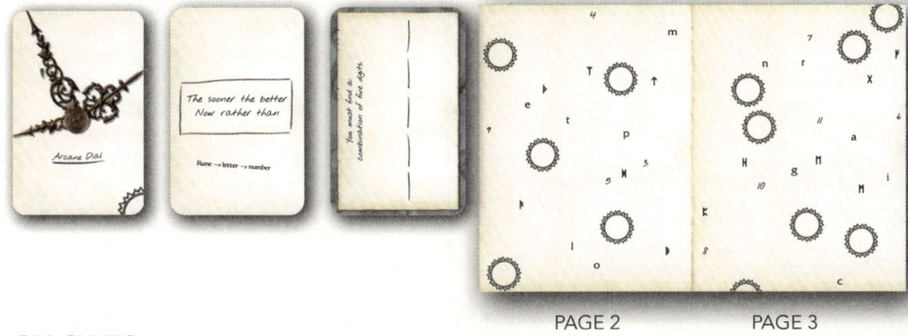

GM CLUES:

❶ You know how an Arcane Dial works, but this one is more complex and requires additional actions.

❷ Answering the riddle on card 37 might help determine the right order for the solution.

METHOD:

The heroes already understand the concept of an Arcane Dial, but this time it has three hands. This one requires three steps to turn a rune into a number.

The heroes align the matching element on the Arcane Dial card to start translating the symbols into letters, and then the letters into numbers as indicated on card 37. The players will know they have the correct order of numbers if the corresponding letters spell **LATER**, the answer to the riddle.

SOLUTION:

KEY

$\text{B} = l = 3$
$\text{F} = a = 7$
$\uparrow = t = 4$
$\text{R} = e = 5$
$\text{M} = r = 6$

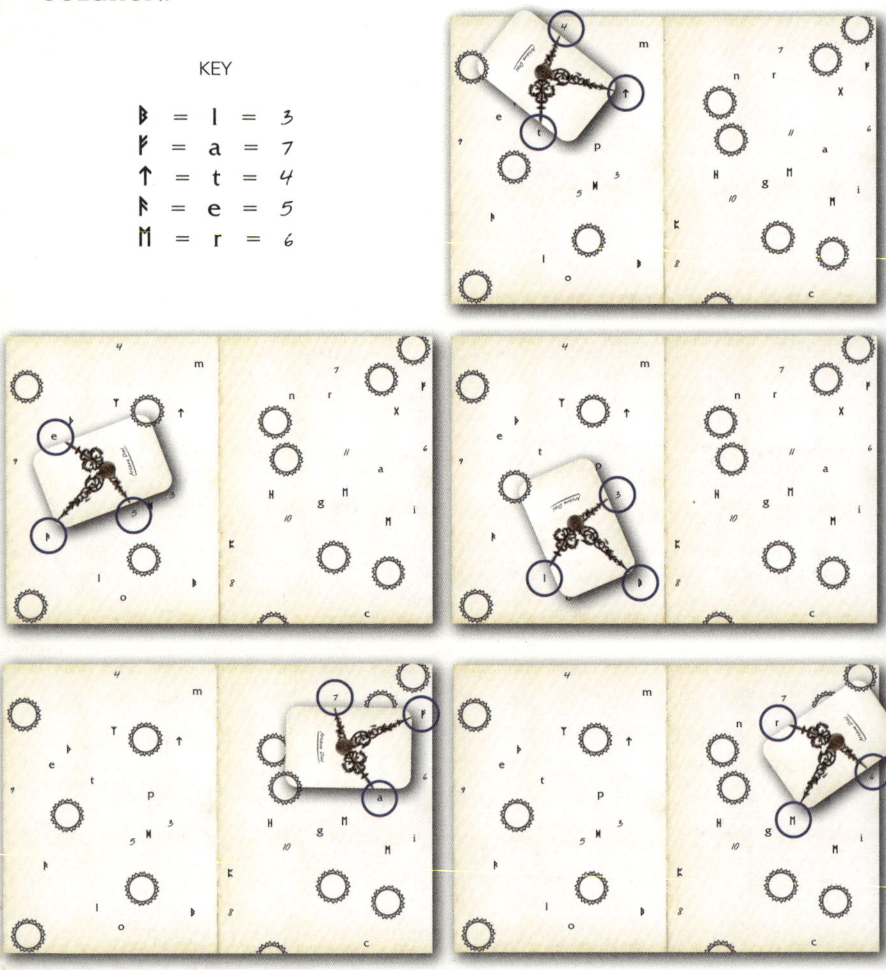

When the heroes find **37456** by solving the word **LATER**, read them this:

"'That's it!' Moroes says happily. 'We've stabilized the Hereafter!'"

GM: Place card 39 on the top box of the Poster.

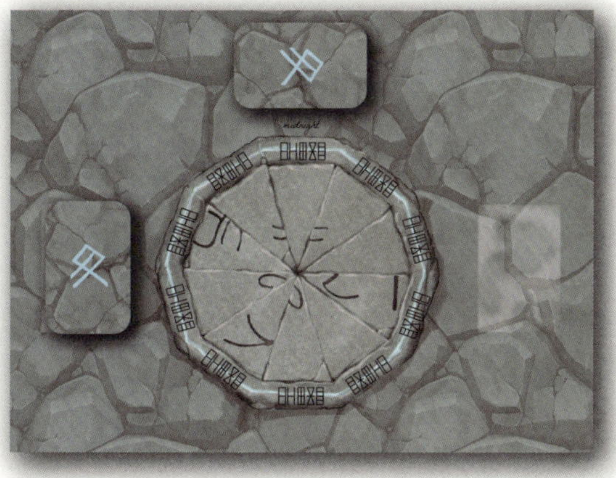

"'The second rune is in place! That means all that's left is the Present. We shouldn't need the Prism because we are already aligned with the Present! There is only one thing left to do: read the stone. Hurry!'"

GM: Give the heroes card 40.

PUZZLE 9: STABILIZE THE PRESENT

MATERIALS: Card 40 and Poster

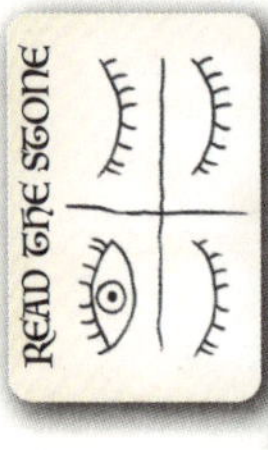

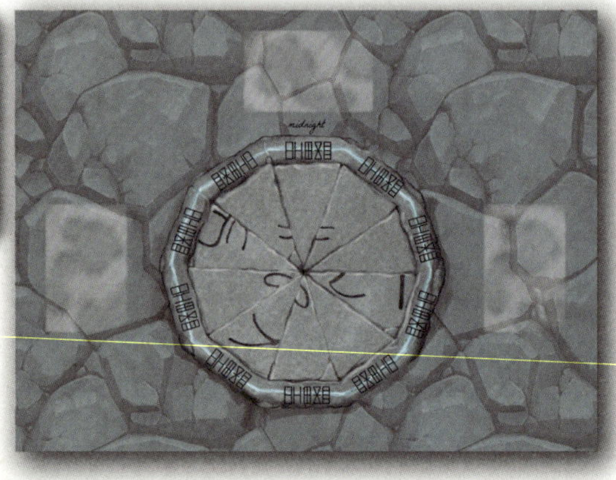

GM CLUES:

1. What do you have that is made of stone?
2. The solution may very well have been right in front of your nose for some time. After all, it is something engraved in the Present.
3. Have you taken a close look at the frame around the arcane interface?
4. Have you tried eliminating parts of the inscriptions on it?

METHOD:

The heroes realize that what they need to look at are the features on the frame around the arcane interface.

Using card 39, they eliminate the redundant parts of each symbol to read its top left quadrant and discover the hidden message: **CLOSE**.

SOLUTION:

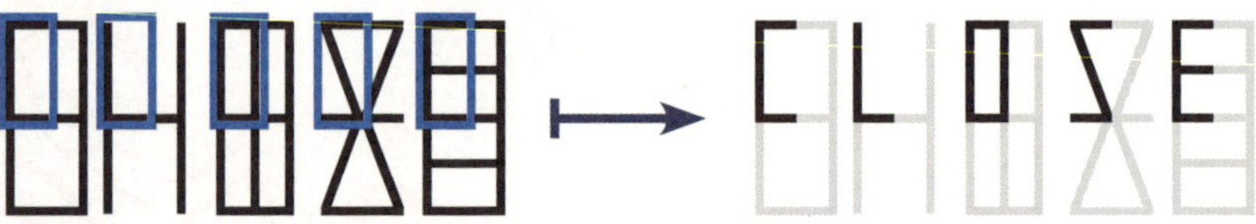

Once the heroes have found the solution, the GM reads the following text aloud.

"The third rune appears on the arcane interface."

GM: Place card 41 on the right box on the Poster.

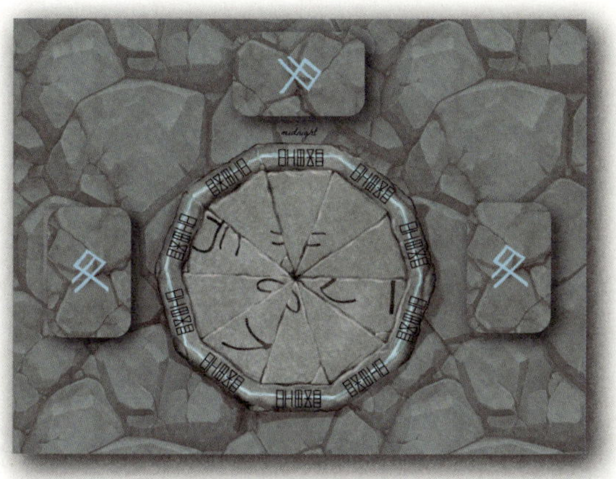

"The stone tablet emits a bright light before releasing a powerful wave of energy that throws you to the ground.

'Well done!' says Moroes as Karazhan stops shaking. 'Thanks to your insight, you have saved Karazhan and its placement in time.'

Calm returns to Karazhan once again. You are teleported to the foot of the tower, free to return home."

GM notes

RULE BOOK

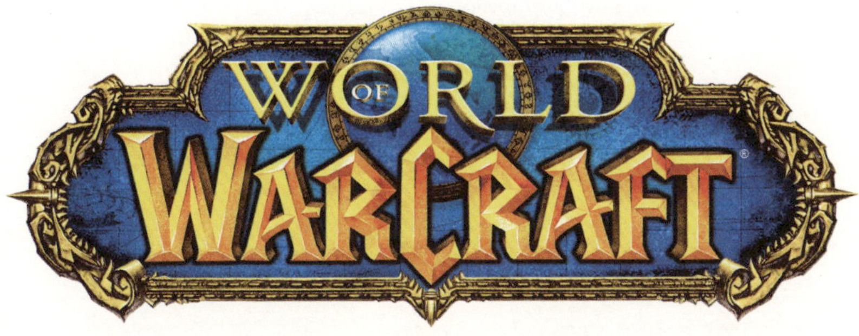

UNSHACKLED

AN ESCAPE ROOM BOX

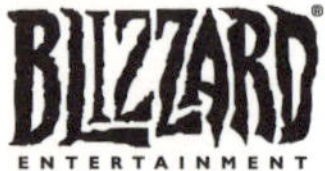

Additional Puzzles by: Helen Cheng
Edited by: Allison Avalon Irons, Chloe Fraboni
Designed by: Betsy Peterschmidt
Produced by: Derek Rosenberg
Lore Consultation by: Sean Copeland

BLIZZARD ENTERTAINMENT
Vice President, Consumer Products: Matthew Beecher
Director, Consumer Products, Publishing: Byron Parnell
Associate Publishing Manager: Derek Rosenberg
Director, Manufacturing: Anna Wan
Senior Director, Story and Franchise Development: David Seeholzer
Senior Producer: Brianne Messina
Lead Editor: Chloe Fraboni
Editor: Allison Avalon Irons
Book Art & Design Manager: Betsy Peterschmidt
Historian Supervisor: Sean Copeland
Senior Historian: Justin Parker
Associate Historian: Madi Buckingham

TITAN BOOKS
A division of Titan Publishing Group Ltd
144 Southwark Street. London SE1 0UP
www.titanbooks.com
Find us on Facebook: www.facebook.com/titanbooks
Follow us on Twitter: @TitanBooks
A CIP catalogue record for this title is available
from the British Library.

ISBN barcode: 978-1-7890-9888-4
Manufactured in China

Print run 10 9 8 7 6 5 4 3 2 1

RULE BOOK

World of Warcraft: Unshackled allows you to create an escape room experience with family or friends in your own home. The players will take the roles of heroes from the Horde or the Alliance, trapped together by some malevolent force. They will need to find clues and solve puzzles within a limited time frame by searching the game space and working together. The escape room is run by a Game Master (GM) who will hide the clues, validate answers, and help the players if they get stuck. If the players can solve all puzzles before the allotted time runs out, they will emerge from the room victorious! This boxed set contains three scenarios set in three fan-favorite *Warcraft* locations. The scenarios are arranged in ascending order of difficulty.

CONTENTS

155 cards
6 class cards
1 foldable prism
1 poster
1 rule book
1 scenario book

1 Apprentice's Notebook
3 found documents
3 soundtracks (one for each scenario) downloadable from the included QR codes

DURATION

Each scenario takes approximately **5** to **10 minutes** for the Game Master to set up. A game lasts **60 minutes** (Scenarios 1 and 2) or **75 minutes** (Scenario 3). The game time will be measured by the downloaded soundtrack. Using a watch, clock, or stopwatch alongside the soundtrack can also be helpful.

NUMBER OF PLAYERS AND ADJUSTABLE DIFFICULTY

The game was created for 3 to 6 participants: one Game Master and up 5 to heroes. If there are only 2 or 3 heroes, the GM may make the search for the puzzle cards easier or intervene with clues to nudge players in the right direction during the game.

The Game Master can adjust the difficulty of the game with the placement of puzzle cards around the play area (as indicated at the start of each scenario). **To lower the difficulty**, the GM can choose a maximum of 6 cards that they will leave in plain sight, in addition to those indicated in the scenario book. This will make it easier for a smaller group of heroes or beginners to escape the room in the allotted amount of time. **To raise the difficulty**, the GM can hide some or all of the cards that would normally stay visible.

OPTIONAL ADDITION: MYTHIC EVENTS

To challenge seasoned escape room experts, the Game Master may deploy **mythic events**. Mythic events are optional features that significantly increase the difficulty of each scenario. If the GM is feeling extra creative, they can invent other mythic events if they so wish.

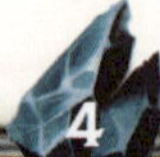

REPLAY

If the players fail to escape the room before the timer ends, the Game Master totals which and how many puzzles were solved. They can then adjust the allotted time for the next try depending on how many puzzles the players had already deciphered:

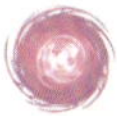 If the heroes have 6 or fewer puzzles to solve, the GM will take 15 minutes off the game time.

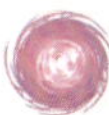 If they have 4 or fewer puzzles to solve, the GM will take 30 minutes off the game time.

To do this, play the soundtrack from the 15- or 30-minute point.

ANATOMY OF A GAME

1. Game participants appoint a Game Master. The GM selects a scenario and reads the accompanying pages in the scenario book.

2. The heroes select class cards or are assigned a class at random by the GM.

3. The heroes leave the gaming area, and the GM begins setting up the escape room according to the scenario book.

4. The GM gathers the needed elements for the scenario from the *World of Warcraft: Unshackled* escape room box.

5. The GM places the required elements and/or cards where they can be seen.

6. The GM hides the puzzle cards for the scenario.

7. The GM sets out paper and pens for the heroes to write with, if desired, and invites the heroes back into the gaming space.

8. The GM reads the introduction from the scenario book.

9. The timer and music start: the heroes begin their daring escape!

10. The heroes search the gaming space for the hidden puzzle cards.

11. The heroes work together to solve the puzzles.

12. The heroes escape the room if they can solve all puzzles within 60 minutes (for Scenarios 1 and 2) or 75 minutes (for Scenario 3).

BEFORE THE GAME BEGINS

There are two types of players: **heroes** and the **Game Master**.

Before the game begins, the players will need to select a Game Master. The other players will be heroes. Heroes cannot access the rule book or the scenario book. The GM must read the rules and the scenario book in their entirety before beginning play. The GM is the one to set up the escape room, apply the rules, hand out cards as rewards when a puzzle is solved, and to help the players if they get stuck. The GM cannot play a scenario they have already run because they will know the answers to the puzzles. However, they can become a hero in a subsequent scenario.

This escape room box includes three scenarios:

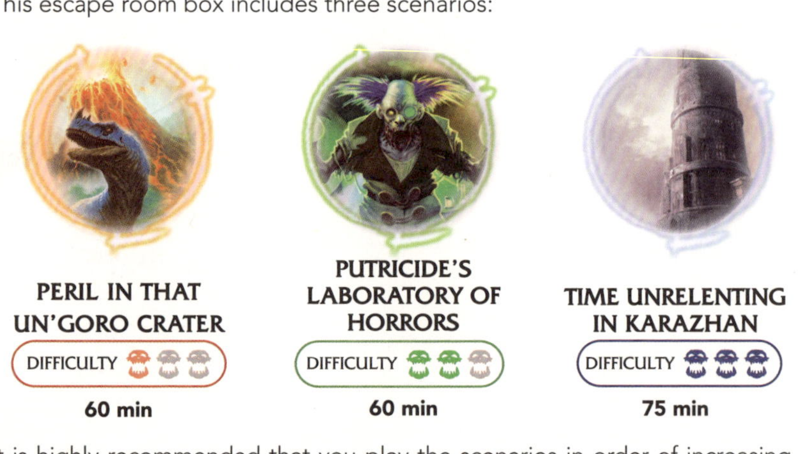

PERIL IN THAT UN'GORO CRATER

DIFFICULTY

60 min

PUTRICIDE'S LABORATORY OF HORRORS

DIFFICULTY

60 min

TIME UNRELENTING IN KARAZHAN

DIFFICULTY

75 min

It is highly recommended that you play the scenarios in order of increasing difficulty.

CLASSES

One of the fundamental features of *World of Warcraft* is its variety of playable classes. In *World of Warcraft: Unshackled*, the heroes will be able to take on the role of their favorite class and escape from mortal peril (or from their living room).

Each class card grants the player a unique power to help them over the course of the game. Each power can be played **once** during one scenario.

Classes can be picked by the players before the game begins or handed out randomly by the Game Master. Each hero will keep the same role throughout the game but can change classes in between scenarios.

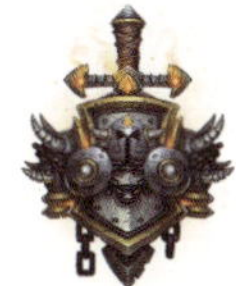

WARRIOR

Rage: The Warrior is always prepared for a fight. Once during a scenario, the Warrior can use their brawn to protect themselves or another player from a hostile effect set off by the GM.

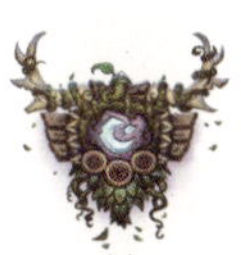

DRUID

Prowl: Once during a scenario, the Druid can ask for one answer to one component of a puzzle and the GM must answer truthfully. However, the use of the Druid's ability costs one victory point.

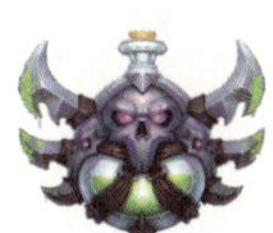

ROGUE

Tricks of the Trade: Once during a scenario, the Rogue can ask for an additional clue about a puzzle without impacting the victory points tally.

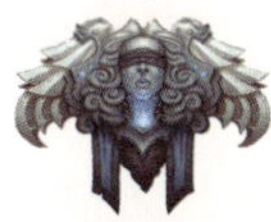

PRIEST

Purify: The Priest can remove a hostile effect from a teammate once during a scenario.

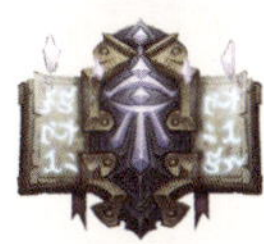

MAGE

Time Warp: Once during a scenario, the Mage can add an extra 5 minutes to the game timer for the whole team.

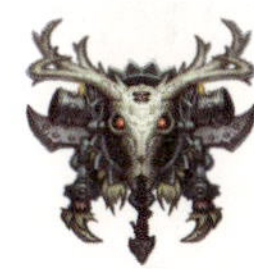

HUNTER

Eyes of the Beast: Once during a scenario, the Hunter can immediately find a hidden element by asking the GM for the location of a card or sheet they're missing from the puzzle their team is working on.

FACTIONS: A CYCLE OF HATRED

In addition to their class, each hero decides if they are **Horde** or **Alliance**.

Since the beginning of *Warcraft*, the Horde and the Alliance have been at odds. While they can occasionally come together for a common cause, they always end up back at each other's throats. To represent this, *World of Warcraft: Unshackled* features a competitive mechanic: the **Cycle of Hatred**.

The heroes all want to do their respective factions proud. Throughout the game, the GM should make a note of who solved which puzzle according to their faction. If puzzles are solved collaboratively, each faction gains one point. Once the scenario is complete and the heroes have escaped the room, the faction with the most correct answers is considered the "true winner."

The Cycle of Hatred is an **optional** feature and does not change the difficulty of the scenarios.

ESCAPE ROOM RULES

First, the Game Master decides on the gaming area. Before beginning the escape room, the players should understand the boundaries in which the game will be held. The GM should also indicate which places or items are out of bounds, such as restrooms, drawers, or cabinets. Neither the GM nor the heroes will have to search outside the designated places or touch the out-of-bounds items.

Note: As time starts to run out and the tension builds, players can sometimes be rough with the gaming area during their desperate search. While the players do need to escape the room, it is important to prevent any real accidents or damage. The GM should warn players in advance if there are any fragile items or unsteady furniture within the gaming area. These items are considered to be out of bounds despite being within the gaming area. It is advisable to remove any delicate items from the gaming area, such as glass or breakable objects. The GM can finalize and adjust these safety rules with the owners of the space they play in. The out-of-bounds places and items should be indicated by the GM before the players leave the room and again before the timer starts (and during the game if needed).

Example: If a piece of furniture hosts a series of fragile miniatures or a spiny cactus, these will be declared out of bounds.

The gaming area should be large enough to hold all the players and contain enough places to hide all the cards. If desired, the GM can offer to add a second room to the gaming space. The players can come and go as they wish between both spaces. It is recommended that you avoid using bathrooms and the kitchen as water could damage the game materials. Once the boundaries and safety rules are established, the heroes leave the gaming space so the GM can hide the cards.

There are several types of materials in each scenario:

- **Class cards** to remind each player of their power.

- **Puzzles cards** that must be manipulated to solve their mysteries.

- **Unique rule cards** that correspond to the flavor of the scenario, like the **bloodpetals** for Scenario 1 or the **Temporary Serum** for Scenario 2.

- **The Apprentice's Notebook** and **found documents** containing cryptic information.

The heroes may also be given special materials that the GM will explain.

PLAYERS SHOULD NOT READ BEYOND THIS POINT.

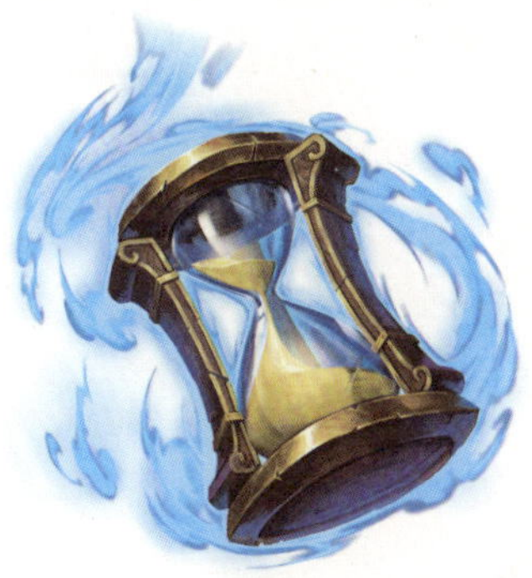

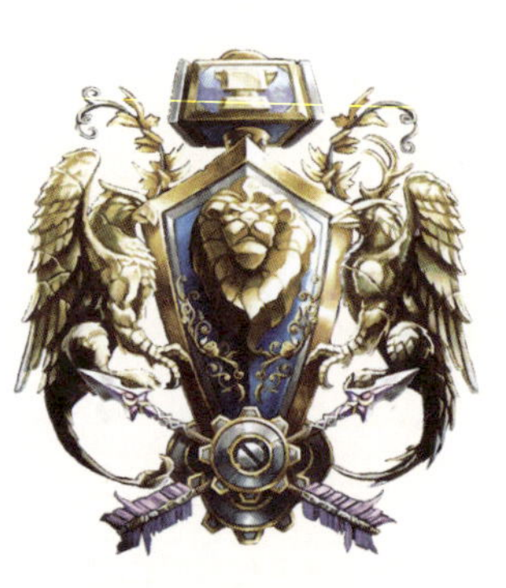 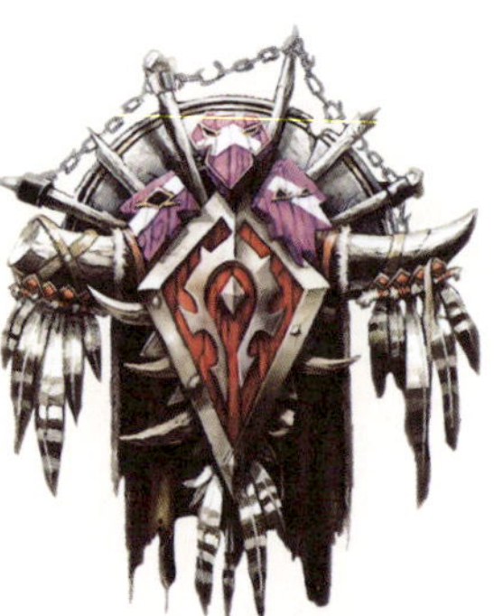

① SETTING UP – PART ONE

The Game Master gathers all the needed elements as indicated in the scenario book.

The scenario book indicates which card numbers are needed for each scenario. The GM separates the cards into several sets, as instructed.

② SETTING UP – PART TWO

The GM puts the cards that should remain visible in plain sight, such as on a table.

③ SETTING UP – PART THREE

The GM hides the rest of the puzzle cards in the gaming space. It is recommended they start with the cards that should be well hidden and finish with the remaining cards.

See hints on hiding cards in the Advice section.

④ SETTING UP – PART FOUR

Once everything is set up, the GM invites the players back into the gaming space and repeats the boundaries and out-of-bounds exceptions. If desired, the GM gives out some blank sheets of paper and pencils for the heroes to try out ideas on.

⑤ INTRODUCTION

The GM reads the scenario's introduction out loud. They can reveal the back of a card from their hand to show the heroes what to search for.

⑥ THE ESCAPE STARTS

The GM starts the 60- or 75-minute timer either by playing the soundtrack or with a watch or clock. In the case of the soundtrack, the volume should be loud enough so that all players can hear it but not so loud that it would hinder communication. If the GM uses a clock, they should announce at what time the game will stop, then announce the remaining time every 10 minutes, and then each minute for the last 5 minutes. They will count down the last 30 seconds.

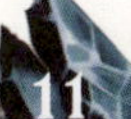

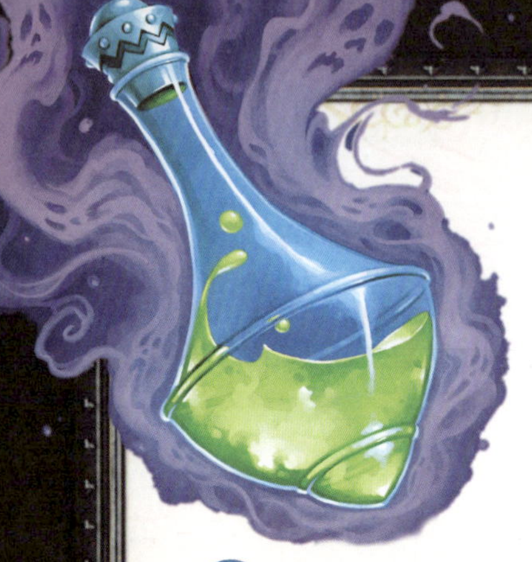

⑦ SEARCHING AND CLUES

The heroes search the game area. If needed, the GM can remind the players of the boundaries of the area. The heroes should announce their discoveries and display the found cards on a table or another visible surface so that everyone can access them.

⑧ SOLUTION

The heroes can try to solve any puzzle at any time during the game. They likely will find clues for puzzle cards they have not found yet. The heroes should offer their solution by showing the puzzle and/or clue card(s) and speaking the answer aloud or drawing/tracing it with their finger if needed. If the proposed answer is correct, the GM can validate it and provide a reward (a new card) or new information.

⑨ ENDGAME

The game is over when the heroes solve the last puzzle or when the timer runs out. If the heroes do not finish the scenario in the allotted time, they can still keep on playing to conclude the adventure if the GM allows it.

VICTORY POINTS

If using the Cycle of Hatred rules, the GM totals the points per faction at the end of the game. To do so, they start from a 20-point total and dock one point for each time the team needed clues. This will allow the heroes to get a grasp on their performance.

20 Points	15–19 Points	10–14 Points	5–9 Points	0–4 Points
LEGENDARY HEROES	DEFENDERS OF AZEROTH	ABLE ADVENTURERS	APPRENTICES	NPCS

ADVICE

TIPS FOR HIDING CARDS

Generally, cards should be accessible without strenuous effort: avoid forcing players to lift a heavy object or reach for an elevated place beyond arm's reach.

In the same spirit, cards should not be impossible to find. Do not slip them into books, in between documents, or inside full drawers.

If the GM chooses to hide a card under furniture, players should be able to catch a small part of the card to slide it toward themselves. The GM must leave a small part of the card exposed for the players to see and must not use furniture to hold the card in place.

It is completely acceptable to bring new items into the room to increase the number of hiding possibilities, if the players agree. Decorations, boxes, books, chairs, or cushions will allow the GM to hide cards more efficiently. Be mindful that if the players have already seen the room where the game is being held, they might notice those new items and search there first.

CHALLENGING HIDING PLACES

- The top of furniture is a good hiding spot, provided it is both safe and accessible. Cards do not have to be visible if the players can touch them.

- Setting a card inside a lampshade is a particularly challenging hiding place.

- Hiding a card behind a picture or a mirror can be difficult, but it will be just as difficult to find. The best technique is to slide the card between the frame and the wall. The weight of the frame should hold the card in place.

- Some tables include extensions that provide perfect flat surfaces for hiding cards.

- Slipping a card underneath several books in a bookcase can make it very difficult to see at a glance.

- Players are less likely to check areas closer to where they entered the room.

EASIER HIDING SPACES

- On top of or behind game consoles, computers, or stereo equipment
- Underneath flowerpots or inside plants
- Underneath or between chair or couch cushions
- Underneath tablecloths or other visible objects
- On a window ledge (particularly if you are playing at night or with the curtains drawn)
- In the pockets of unworn clothes

Each room offers new hiding possibilities to add to the experience. If accessible and available, try to play each scenario in a different room.

HELPING THE PLAYERS

Over the course of the game, the heroes might mistakenly refer to clues from different puzzles or become completely stuck. The Game Master should also maintain a sense of fun in the game by clarifying the situation for the heroes.

If the GM notices the heroes are at a loss on a puzzle and the game is lagging, they can give a clue about an unsolved puzzle. At a normal pace, the players should solve half the puzzles by the 30-minute mark in all scenarios. If the players are falling behind, the GM should help them.

To that end, the GM might point to a card that has not been found yet, or they can indicate that some card has no place in a particular puzzle. Some of these clues are mentioned in the scenario book as well.

OUTSIDE REFERENCES

The players might feel tempted to consult their phone, computer, or a handy book to find information. The players should ideally refrain from using outside references for answers.

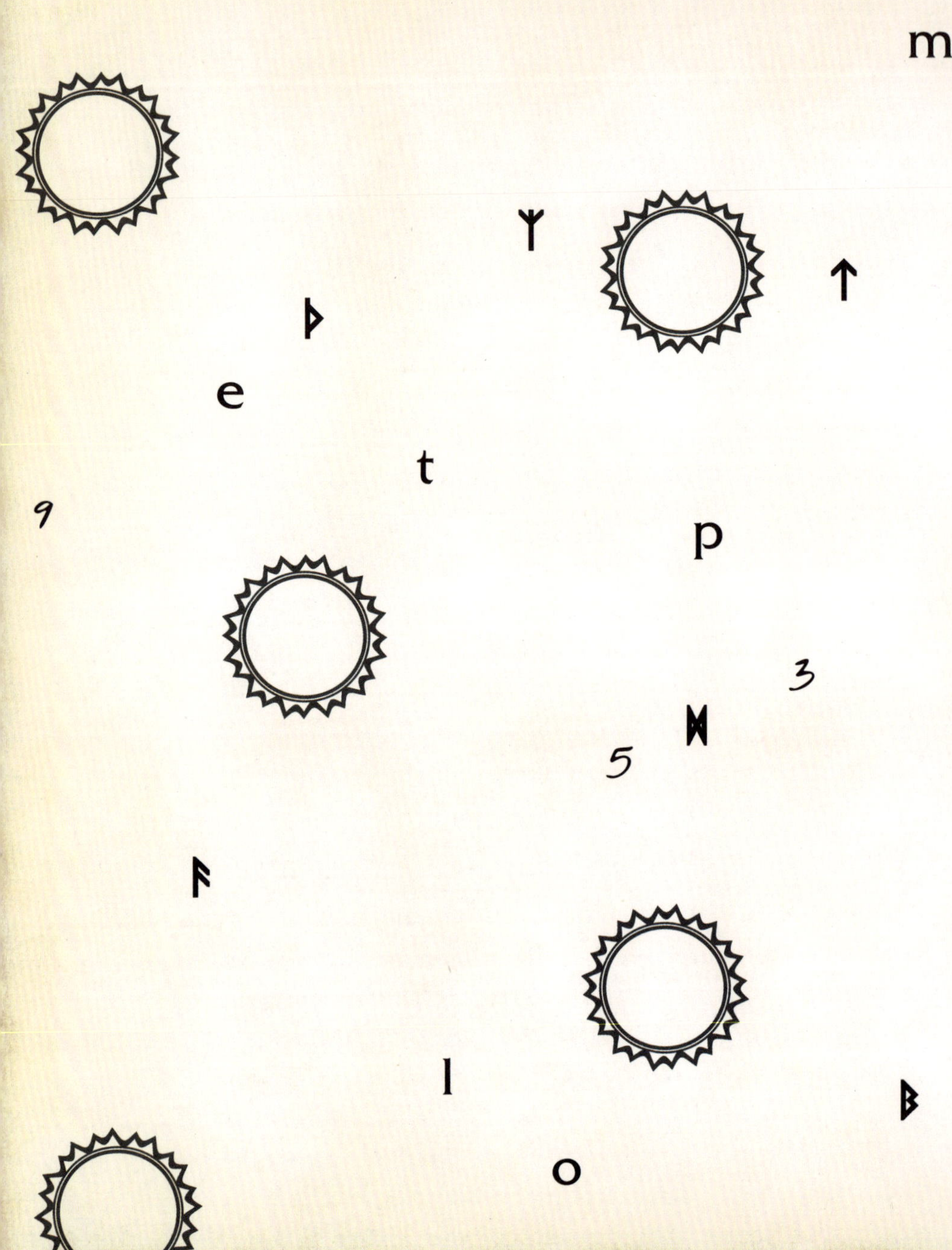

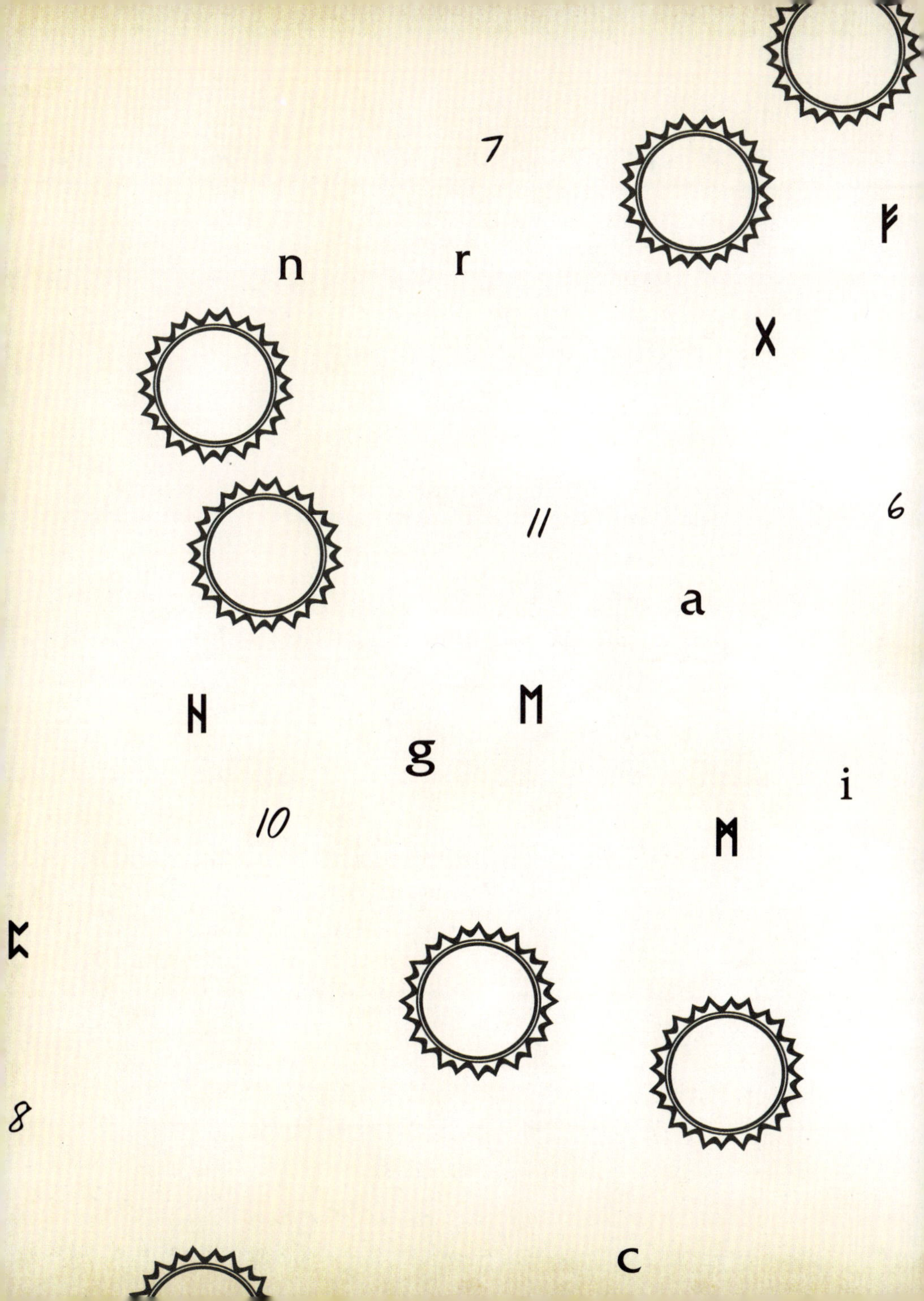
7
r
n
6
//
a
n
g
i
10
8
c

TRACING RUNES

None of it makes any
sense at all!

Do I have the spine
to see this through?

"Leafing through the storm and the mountains

Guarded by the howling wolves;

Intimacy of creatures under the starry sky;

Lost nation chilled to the bone"

Our eyes deceive us
too easily . . .

PERFORM
AN ADVANCED
RITUAL

For all

Altars come in threes to ensure stability. Each is adorned with six candles. Chance has no place here, as the altars are linked together; the first two measurements always tell us the third. But you must look carefully.

After size comes color

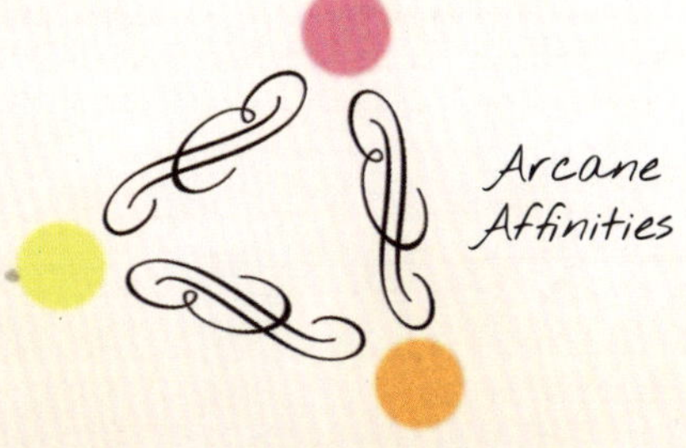

Arcane Affinities

CONJURATIONS

Earth →

Air →

Water →

Fire →

PRISM OF TIME: INSTRUCTIONS FOR USE

Karazhan is an incredible source of magic, but one that must be contained. To do this, Medivh created an arcane interface and the Prism of Time to control it. When used correctly, they keep Karazhan's place in the timeline stable: the Past, Present, and Hereafter.

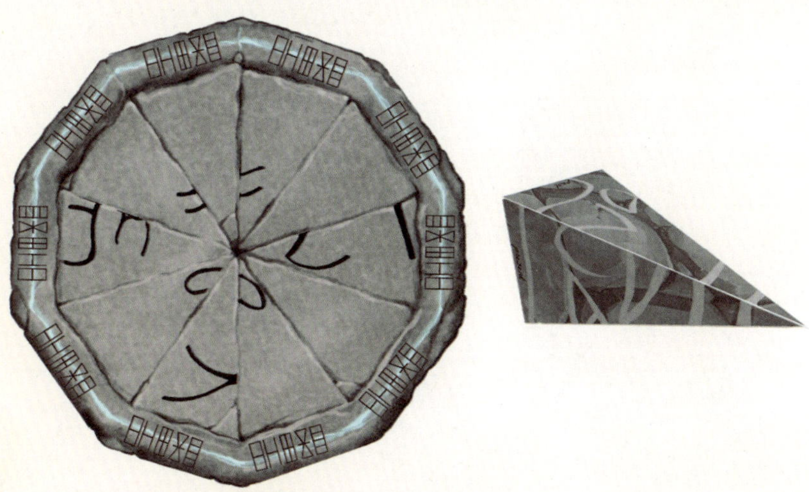

You must first align yourself with the desired timeline in order to stabilize it. Place the prism and follow the instructions. Find the right letter of power to say. You just need to look carefully.

Notes

Notes

Notes